SCHOLASTIC

CLOSE READING

FICTION

AGES 11+

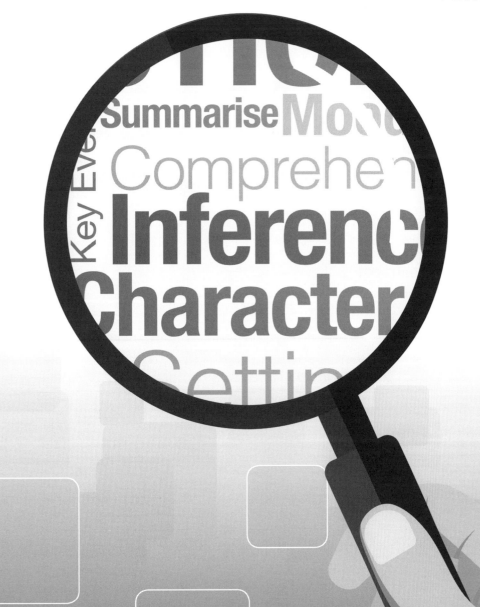

Scholastic Education, an imprint of Scholastic Ltd
Book End, Range Road, Witney, Oxfordshire, OX29 0YD
Registered office: Westfield Road, Southam, Warwickshire CV47 0RA
www.scholastic.co.uk
© 2016, Scholastic Inc. © 2019, Scholastic Ltd
1 2 3 4 5 6 7 8 9   9 0 1 2 3 4 5 6 7 8

British Library Cataloguing-in-Publication Data
A catalogue record for this book is available from the British Library.
ISBN 978-1407-18280-3

Printed and bound by Ashford Colour Press

Author
Marcia Miller, Martin Lee
Editorial
Rachel Morgan, Louise Titley, Jane Wood and Rebecca Rothwell
Cover and Series Design
Scholastic Design Team: Nicolle Thomas, Neil Salt and Alice Duggan
Illustrations
Doug Jones, Kelly Kennedy, Michael Moran and Jason Robinson

UK Revised Edition. Originally published by Scholastic Inc, 557 Broadway, New York, NY 10012 (ISBN: 978-0-545-79389-6)

Contents

Texts and Questions

Character

Point of View

Setting/Mood

Key Events & Details

Sequence of Events

Conflict & Resolution

Context Clues

Compare & Contrast

Make Inferences

Summarise

Introduction

Texts For Close Reading and Deep Comprehension

Close reading involves careful study of a short text passage to build a deep, critical understanding of the text. By developing children's comprehension and higher-order thinking skills, you can help them make sense of the world.

> "A significant body of research links the close reading of complex text – whether the student is a struggling reader or advanced – to significant gains in reading proficiency, and finds close reading to be a key component of college and career readiness."
> (Partnership for Assessment of Readiness for College and Careers, 2012, p7)

Reading and Re-Reading For Different Purposes

The texts in *Close Reading* are carefully selected and deliberately short. This focuses children on purposeful reading, re-reading and responding. They learn about the topic through rich vocabulary development and deep comprehension.

1st Reading — PREPARE AND READ
2nd Reading — READ CLOSELY
3rd Reading — DISCUSS
4th Reading — WRITE

Children re-read and analyse the text through questioning to explore:

* text structure and features
* key ideas and details
* connections/conclusions
* predictions/inferences
* words and phrases in context.

Children actively respond to the text using:

* higher-order thinking skills
* paired discussion
* written responses.

Text Marking: A Powerful Active-Reading Strategy

To improve their comprehension of literary texts, children must actively engage with the material. Careful and consistent text marking by hand is one valuable way to accomplish this. The true goal of teaching text marking is to help children internalise an effective close-reading strategy, not to have them show how many marks they can make on a page. Text-marking skills are encouraged in each passage.

Introduction

About the Texts and Questions

This book provides 20 reproducible texts that address ten key reading-comprehension skills:

- Character
- Point of View
- Setting/Mood
- Key Events & Details
- Sequence of Events
- Conflict & Resolution
- Context Clues
- Compare & Contrast
- Make Inferences
- Summarise

    The contents pages detail the skills and genres covered as well as the Lexile score (see page 7). The passages are stand-alone texts that can be used in any order you choose by individuals, pairs, groups or the whole class. (See page 9 for a close-reading routine to model.)

    Following each passage is a reproducible 'Questions' page of text-dependent comprehension questions.

    Answers are provided. They include sample text marking and answers. Encourage children to self-assess and revise their answers as you review the text markings together. This approach encourages discussion, comparison, extension, reinforcement and correlation to other reading skills.

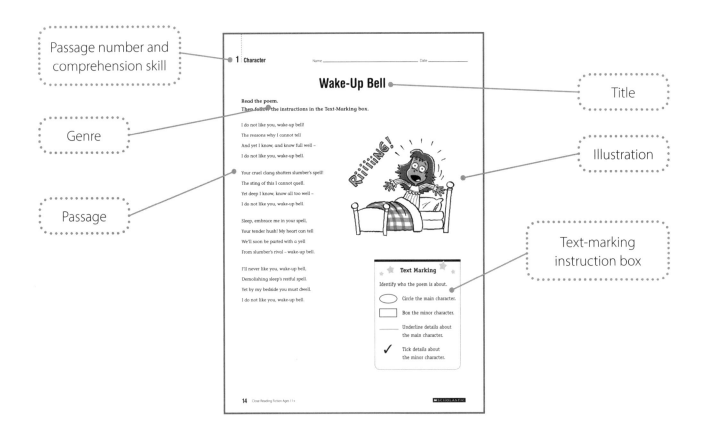

SCHOLASTIC

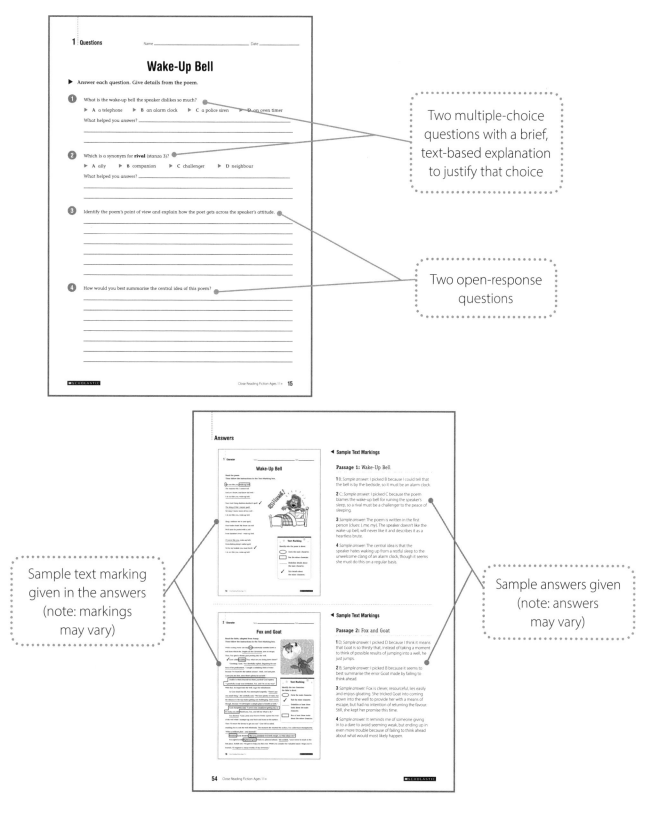

Two multiple-choice questions with a brief, text-based explanation to justify that choice

Two open-response questions

Sample text marking given in the answers (note: markings may vary)

Sample answers given (note: answers may vary)

Lexiles

The Lexile Framework® finds the right books for children by measuring readers and texts on the same scale. Lexile measures are the global standard in reading assessment and are accurate for all ages, including first- and second-language learners. The Lexile scores fall within the ranges recommended for children aged 11+. (The poem on page 14 does not include a Lexile score because poetry is excluded from Lexile measurements.)

Introduction

Comprehension Skill Summary Cards

Comprehension Skill Summary Cards are provided on pages 11–13 to help support the children. The terms in bold are the same ones the children will identify as they mark the text.

Give children the relevant card before providing them with the text passage. Discuss the skill together to ensure that children understand it. Encourage the children to use the cards as a set of reading aids to refer to whenever they read any type of fiction text or display the cards in your classroom.

Comprehension Skill
Character

Characters take part in the events of the story. A character can be a person, an animal or a thing.

- Read for details that describe each character.
- Notice differences among characters so you can tell them apart.
- Notice whether and how a character changes or learns during the story.

A story may have a **main character** and one or more **minor characters**.

- The main character is the most important character in the story.
- A minor character is not the focus of the story.

Comprehension Skill
Setting/Mood

The **setting** of a story tells *where* and *when* the story takes place. The setting can help create the **mood** or feeling of the story.

Read for details that tell where a story takes place.

- It can be a *real* place.
- It can be an *imaginary* place.

Read for details that tell when a story takes place.

- It might be set in the *present* (now).
- It might be set in the *past* (long ago).
- It might be set in the *future* (years from now).

Comprehension Skill
Key Events & Details

Events are the actions or things that happen in a story. The events build interest and move the story along. But not all events have the same effect on the story.

As you read, think about which actions or things are **key events** and which are **details**.

- A key event is important to the theme or big idea of the story.
- Details tell more about a key event. Details may answer questions, such as *Who? Where? What? When? Why?* or *How?*

Tips and Suggestions

- The text-marking process is adaptable. While numbering, boxing, circling and underlining are the most common methods, you can personalise the strategy for your class. You might ask the children to use letters to mark text; for example, write 'MC' to indicate a main character, 'D' to mark a detail, or '1st' for first person and '3rd' for third person. Whichever technique you use, focus on the need for consistency of marking.

- You may wish to extend the text-marking strategy by asking the children to identify other aspects of writing, such as confusing words, expressions or idioms. You can also encourage them to write their own notes and questions in the margins.

 SCHOLASTIC

Teaching Routine for Close Reading and Text Marking

Here is one suggested routine to use Close Reading and Text Marking in the classroom.

Preview

- **Engage prior knowledge** of the passage topic and its genre. Help children link it to similar topics or examples of the genre they may have read.
- **Identify the reading skill** for which children will be marking the text. Display or distribute the relevant Comprehension Skill Summary Card and review these together. (See Comprehension Skill Summary Cards, page 8.)

Model *(for the first passage, to familiarise children with the process)*

- **Display the passage** and provide children with their own copy. Look at the text together by reading the title and looking at the illustration.
- **Draw attention to the markings** children will use to enhance their understanding of the passage. Link the text-marking box to the Comprehension Skill Summary Card for clarification.
- **Read aloud the passage** as children follow along. Guide children to think about the featured skill and to note any questions they may have on sticky notes.
- **Mark the text together.** Begin by numbering the paragraphs. Then discuss the choices you make when marking the text, demonstrating and explaining how various text elements support the skill. Check that children understand how to mark the text using the icons and graphics shown in the text-marking box.

Read

- **Display each passage for a shared reading experience.** Do a quick read of the passage together to familiarise the children with it. Then read it together a second time, pausing as necessary to answer questions, draw connections or clarify words as needed. Then read the passage once more, this time with an eye to the text features described in the text-marking box.
- **Invite children to offer ideas for additional markings.** These might include noting unfamiliar vocabulary, an idiom or phrase they may not understand, or an especially interesting, unusual or important detail they want to remember. Model how to use sticky notes, coloured pencils, highlighters or question marks.

Respond

- **Ask the children to read the passage independently.** This fourth reading is intended to allow the children to mark the text themselves. It will also prepare them to discuss the piece and offer their views about it.
- **Ask the children to answer the questions on the companion questions page.** Encourage them to look back at their text markings and other text evidence. This will help the children to provide complete and supported responses.

National Curriculum Correlation

	Passages
• reading a wide range of fiction, including short stories	1–20
• learning new vocabulary, relating it explicitly to known vocabulary and understanding it with the help of context and dictionaries	1, 3, 4, 6, 7, 9, 13, 14, 15, 17, 20
• making inferences and referring to evidence in the text	1–20
• knowing the purpose, audience for and context of the writing and drawing on this knowledge to support comprehension	1, 11, 12, 17
• knowing how language, including figurative language, vocabulary choice, grammar, text structure and organisational features, presents meaning	2, 4, 5, 6, 8, 20
• studying setting, plot and characterisation, and the effects of these	1, 2, 5, 6, 7, 8, 9, 10

■SCHOLASTIC

Character

Characters take part in the events of the story. A character can be a person, an animal or a thing.

- Read for details that describe each character.
- Notice differences among characters so you can tell them apart.
- Notice whether and how a character changes or learns during the story.

A story may have a **main character** and one or more **minor characters**.

- The main character is the most important character in the story.
- A minor character is not the focus of the story.

Point of View

Knowing *who* is telling a story gives you its **point of view**. What you learn in the story comes through that point of view. Authors usually use one of two points of view.

- **First-person** point of view has a character *in* the story telling it. In first-person stories, readers learn about events from that character's point of view. Look for words like *I*, *me* and *we*.
- **Third-person** point of view has someone *outside* the story telling it. That person is the **narrator**. In third-person stories, readers learn the thoughts, actions and feelings of many characters. Look for words like *he*, *she* and *they*.

Setting/Mood

The **setting** of a story tells *where* and *when* the story takes place. The setting can help create the **mood** or feeling of the story.

Read for details that tell where a story takes place.

- It can be a *real* place.
- It can be an *imaginary* place.

Read for details that tell when a story takes place.

- It might be set in the *present* (now).
- It might be set in the *past* (long ago).
- It might be set in the *future* (years from now).

Key Events & Details

Events are the actions or things that happen in a story. The events build interest and move the story along. But not all events have the same effect on the story.

As you read, think about which actions or things are **key events** and which are **details**.

- A key event is important to the theme or big idea of the story.
- Details tell more about a key event. Details may answer questions, such as *Who*? *Where*? *What*? *When*? *Why*? or *How*?

Sequence of Events

In most stories, events happen in a certain order or **sequence**. Some events happen in the *beginning* of the story. Other things happen in the *middle*. The story finishes with events that happen at the *end*.

- As you read, think about the sequence of events. This helps you follow the story. Picture the events in your mind to help you remember the sequence.

- **Signal words** give clues about the sequence of events. (Examples: *before*, *first*, *second*, *next*, *then*, *now*, *later*, *after* and *finally*; as well as specific dates and times.)

Conflict & Resolution

Good stories have a **plot**. The plot is the set of key events that move the story along. Most stories present a problem and how it gets solved. This relationship is called **conflict and resolution**.

- A conflict is a form of trouble, problem or disagreement.

- A resolution is the way the conflict gets solved.

- **Signal words** are clues to a conflict and its resolution. (Examples for conflicts: *question*, *challenge*, *dilemma*, *puzzle*, *need* and *trouble*. Examples for resolutions: *answer*, *result*, *idea*, *plan*, *reason*, *solution*, *solve*, *improve* and *fix*.)

Context Clues

Authors may use words you may not know. But nearby words or sentences can offer clues about the meaning of an unknown word.

- **Context** refers to all the words and sentences around an unknown word.

- **Context clues** are hints that can help you work out a word's meaning. As you read, search for related words, such as synonyms, antonyms, explanations or examples in nearby text. Link these clues to the unknown word to understand it.

Compare & Contrast

Authors often discuss people, places, things or ideas by describing how they are alike and ways they differ.

- To **compare** means to tell how two or more things are alike.

- To **contrast** means to tell how two or more things are different.

- Comparing and contrasting help you understand a story's ideas, its plot, its characters and its message.

- **Signal words** give clues that help you compare and contrast. (Examples for comparing: *both*, *too*, *like*, *also* and *in the same way*. Examples for contrasting: *but*, *only*, *however*, *unlike* and *different*.)

Make Inferences

Authors may hint at an idea without stating it directly. But they usually include enough detail so readers can use what they already know about a topic to 'read between the lines' and work out a hidden message.

- **Text clues** are words or details that help you work out an unstated idea.
- You **make an inference** by combining text clues with what you already know to form a likely conclusion or 'educated guess'.

Summarise

As you read, check that you understand and can recall the key elements of a story. Think about how to retell the important parts in your own words. Leave out minor details and get to the point.

- The **topic** or **theme** of a story is its focus – what it is mainly about.
- **Key details** add more information and support the story's theme.
- A **summary** briefly restates the theme using only the key details. A good summary is short, clear and tells only what is most important.

Name _____ Date _____

Wake-Up Bell

Read the poem.
Then follow the instructions in the Text-Marking box.

I do not like you, wake-up bell!

The reasons why I cannot tell

And yet I know, and know full well –

I do not like you, wake-up bell.

Your cruel clang shatters slumber's spell!

The sting of this I cannot quell.

Yet deep I know, know all too well –

I do not like you, wake-up bell.

Sleep, embrace me in your spell,

Your tender hush! My heart can tell

We'll soon be parted with a yell

From slumber's rival – wake-up bell.

I'll never like you, wake-up bell,

Demolishing sleep's restful spell.

Yet by my bedside you must dwell.

I do not like you, wake-up bell.

Text Marking

Identify who the poem is about.

◯   Circle the main character.

▢   Box the minor character.

_____   Underline details about
the main character.

✓   Tick details about
the minor character.

Name _____ Date _____

Wake-Up Bell

▶ **Answer each question. Give details from the poem.**

1 What is the wake-up bell the speaker dislikes so much?

▶ **A** a telephone ▶ **B** an alarm clock ▶ **C** a police siren ▶ **D** an oven timer

What helped you answer? _____

_____

_____

2 Which is a synonym for **rival** (stanza 3)?

▶ **A** ally ▶ **B** companion ▶ **C** challenger ▶ **D** neighbour

What helped you answer? _____

_____

_____

3 Identify the poem's point of view and explain how the poet gets across the speaker's attitude.

_____

_____

_____

_____

_____

_____

4 How would you best summarise the central idea of this poem?

_____

_____

_____

_____

_____

_____

_____

_____

Name _____ Date _____

Fox and Goat

Read the fable, adapted from Aesop.
Then follow the instructions in the Text-Marking box.

While seeking water one day, Fox accidentally tumbled down a well from which she, despite all her cleverness, saw no escape. Then, Fox spied a thirsty goat peering into the well.

Goat called sociably, "Fox, what are you doing down there?"

"Greetings, Goat," Fox cheerfully replied, disguising the sad facts of her predicament. "I sought a satisfying drink of water because I've heard it's the tastiest around – fresh, cool and pure. Come join me here, since there's plenty for us both."

Unable to think beyond his thirst, parched Goat replied, "I gratefully accept your invitation, Fox, and I'm on my way!" With that, he leaped into the well, eager for refreshment.

As Goat drank his fill, Fox interrupted urgently. "There's just one small thing," she carefully said. "We have plenty of water, but the distance to the top makes getting out challenging. Don't worry, though, because I've developed a simple plan to benefit us both."

Goat sheepishly said, "I never even considered getting out, so it's lucky you did. Thank you, Fox, and tell me what to do."

Fox directed, "Goat, press your hooves firmly against the wall of the well while I scamper up your back and horns to the surface. Then I'll return the favour to get you out." Goat did as asked, enabling Fox to exit the well effortlessly. The moment she reached the surface, Fox called back triumphantly, "What a brilliant plan – and farewell!"

Panicked, Goat shouted, "But you promised we'd both escape, so what about me?"

Fox sighed at the frightened goat. "Had you planned ahead," she scolded, "you'd never be stuck in the first place, foolish one. I'll agree to help you this once. While you consider the valuable lesson I hope you've learned, I'll engineer a rescue worthy of my cleverness."

Text Marking

Identify the two characters the fable is about.

◯   Circle the main character.

✓   Tick the minor character.

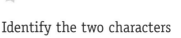   Underline at least three traits about the main character.

▭   Box at least three traits about the minor character.

Fox and Goat

▶ **Answer each question. Give details from the fable.**

1 Think about character. 'Unable to think beyond his thirst' reveals that Goat _____.

▶ **A** easily panics ▶ **B** is too trusting ▶ **C** is very intelligent ▶ **D** reacts before thinking

What helped you answer? _____

_____

_____

_____

2 Which best summarises the moral of this fable?

▶ **A** In union is strength. ▶ **C** Beware a fox in sheep's clothing.

▶ **B** Look before you leap. ▶ **D** Do not attempt too much at once.

What helped you answer? _____

_____

_____

_____

3 Describe the character of Fox, according to details in this fable.

_____

_____

_____

_____

_____

4 Describe a modern-day situation that could be avoided by following the lesson of this fable.

_____

_____

_____

_____

_____

Name _____ Date _____

The Bargain

Read the folktale, adapted from Sholem Aleichem.
Then follow the instructions in the Text-Marking box.

Like everyone in the *shtetl* of Dolna, Velvel was desperately poor.
He eked out a meagre living reading and writing letters for his
neighbours who could not do these things for themselves. In
exchange, they offered him food or cast-off garments. Each night
lowly Velvel worried about how to survive and sought wisdom to
enrich his humble life.

One day, he read a newspaper article about the Feldmans of
Paris, then the world's richest Jewish family; moreover, they were
famously generous to the needy. "All of Dolna is needy," Velvel
thought, and thus decided to seek help from the Feldmans.

It took Velvel two weeks to travel to the grand city of Paris,
during which time he planned ways to convince the Feldmans to
give him money. When the ragged traveller found their mansion,
he nervously knocked on the door. "Greetings!" he said to the
servant who answered. "I am Velvel of Dolna, a poor village far
away. I am here to speak with Mr Feldman on behalf of us all."

The servant ushered Velvel inside, brushed the dust from his
clothes and let him wash his hands and face to prepare to meet
Mr Feldman. The two men drank tea until Mr Feldman asked the
reason for Velvel's visit. "Sir, we offer you something that not even
the wealthiest man can buy. I'm willing to sell you the secret of
eternal life at a price of only 500 rubles." Without hesitation,
Mr Feldman counted out the money and shook Velvel's hand.

"Now that I've paid you," he said, "please reveal your secret."

"Come live in Dolna," Velvel replied, "where no *rich* man has ever died!"

shtetl = any poor close-knit village in
central Europe where Yiddish-speaking
Jews once lived

Text Marking

Determine the story's point of view.

▢ Box signal words that
suggest who tells
the story.

✗ Cross the box that shows
how the story is told.

   ▢ first person

   ▢ third person

⬭ Circle the name
of the main character.

✓ Tick the name of the
minor character.

_____ Underline words or
phrases that describe the
main character.

The Bargain

▶ **Answer each question. Give details from the folktale.**

1 In what way did the Feldmans differ most from the people of Dolna?

▶ **A** The Feldmans were Jewish.   ▶ **C** The Feldmans were wealthy.

▶ **B** The Feldmans had a dog.   ▶ **D** The Feldmans were kind.

What helped you answer? _____

_____

_____

2 Which word is NOT a synonym of the other three?

▶ **A** lowly   ▶ **B** humble   ▶ **C** needy   ▶ **D** eternal

What helped you answer? _____

_____

_____

3 Write a brief character sketch of Velvel, based on this folktale.

_____

_____

_____

_____

_____

_____

_____

4 Make an inference. Why would Mr Feldman give Velvel money for such an unlikely secret?

_____

_____

_____

_____

_____

Becoming B-boys

Read the urban story.

Then follow the instructions in the Text-Marking box.

My b-boy crew began working on dance moves to deal with our overload of energy. We wanted more than just to watch the styling of other b-boys and b-girls. Jett's brother Cato agreed to teach us, which was amazing because he's well-known for his dramatic drops, power moves, freezes and signature flash.

But Cato set the bar very high, nearly impossible. "The essence of hip-hop dancing" he said, "is to defy gravity while acting totally relaxed." Though eager, we had no flow until Cato broke down each move and demonstrated it in slow motion. He assigned stretches and exercises for us. Each day we got a little looser, stronger and smoother; our endurance grew. Eventually we progressed from basic toprock moves to downrock flips, twists and classic moves like the helicopter and worm.

While giving us an essential foundation, Cato insisted on using teamwork, having patience and learning from mistakes. He also modelled how to handle frustration. He was living proof of the b-boy motto: 'Each One Teach One'. Cato learned from his friend, who learned from his cousin. Cato let us borrow his combinations without accusing us of biting. His generosity kept us focused.

After months of hard work, we wanted to strut our stuff like genuine b-boys – out on the streets for passing crowds. Cato helped us develop our own routine and add our unique personal touches.

The afternoon of our b-boy debut was a sunny autumn Saturday. I staked out a spot near a busy underground entrance to ensure a steady flow of traffic. Wearing matching T-shirts, trainers and caps, we lay down a piece of hardboard, set up our music, cranked up the volume and struck our starting pose.

Text Marking

Determine the story's point of view.

☐ Box signal words that suggest who tells the story.

✗ Cross the box that shows how the story is told.

   ☐ first person

   ☐ third person

_____ Underline words or phrases that describe the narrator and his fellow b-boys.

B-BOY TERMS		
	b-boy:	break dancer
	biting:	stealing
	downrock:	floor moves
	toprock:	standing moves

Becoming B-boys

▶ **Answer each question. Give details from the urban story.**

1 Which word is LEAST likely to represent the extra 'b' in **b-boys**?

▶ **A** beat   ▶ **B** biting   ▶ **C** break   ▶ **D** best

What helped you answer? _____

_____

_____

2 To **set the bar very high** (paragraph 2) means to have _____ expectations. Explain why Cato did this.

▶ **A** few   ▶ **B** low   ▶ **C** hopeless   ▶ **D** challenging

_____

_____

_____

3 Why do you think the author chose to tell this story in the first person?

_____

_____

_____

_____

_____

_____

_____

4 Discuss how the narrator and his crew responded to the challenges of learning to break dance.

_____

_____

_____

_____

_____

When Winter Turned Fierce

Read the weather story.
Then follow the instructions in the Text-Marking box.

Winter began early this year and quickly turned fierce. One storm after another kept the ground snow-covered throughout December. Freezing temperatures kept the streets and pavements icy and dangerous. Not only driving, but walking, too, was hazardous. There were power outages and damage from felled trees. Pipes froze and roofs buckled under the added weight. Many, especially the elderly and frail, stayed indoors. Local businesses suffered from the decrease in traffic.

People were generally gloomy as they awoke to grey skies nearly every morning, and became even gloomier once they'd heard about the snarled roads and all the accidents. Even the usually perky weather forecasters were noticeably glum as they announced each new snowstorm heading our way. The mood in town was not good.

But some community members were not at all dispirited by the conditions. Retailers who sold shovels, salt and snow blowers were having a field day. And breakdown companies had all the work they could handle. But it was the neighbourhood children who truly reaped the benefits of the wintry weather. That's because when the pavements and roads iced over, so did the ponds, which were frozen solid enough for skating and sliding on.

Yes, the children were in heaven, the kind of heaven that a frozen pond could provide. They didn't huddle indoors on the days schools had to be closed. No, they did not. On those days, when the adults were down in the dumps, they collected by the largest of our town's ponds and celebrated.

Text Marking

Think about the setting and mood of the story.

☐ Box WHEN it takes place.

⬭ Circle WHERE it takes place.

✗ Cross the box that shows the setting.
  ☐ real
  ☐ imaginary

_____ Underline details that set the mood.

When Winter Turned Fierce

▶ **Answer each question. Give details from the weather story.**

1 What best describes the mood of the town's residents?

　▶ **A** All were miserable thanks to the terrible weather.

　▶ **B** Most profited from the snow and were pleased.

　▶ **C** Some were upbeat while most were unhappy.

　▶ **D** Everyone was in high spirits.

　What helped you answer? _____

　_____

　_____

2 Which might make a person **dispirited** (paragraph 3)?

　▶ **A** completing a hard job　▶ **B** making a friend　▶ **C** seeing a ghost　▶ **D** failing a test

　What helped you answer? _____

　_____

　_____

　_____

3 What inferences can you draw about how weather affects people's moods?

　_____

　_____

　_____

　_____

　_____

4 Explain why the author provides concrete examples of the effects of the snowstorms.

　_____

　_____

　_____

　_____

Name _____ Date _____

The Case

Read the discovery story.
Then follow the instructions in the Text-Marking box.

The skies were clear that autumn day, and the temperature for a long mountain hike was ideal. Our destination was the campsite at Spruce Notch, 15 kilometres away, where food, music, a campfire and companionship awaited us.

We only had to get there, but that task was proving to be a challenge. Although we had the right clothing, the right shoes and the right attitude, the rocky up-and-down trail was exhausting us. With several kilometres still to go, my ankle was bothering me and the hike was becoming harder with each step. Dash had it worse because a blister the size of a ten pence coin was causing him to wince in pain as he trudged. Disheartened and feeling sorry for ourselves, we gladly took the opportunity to rest and soak our feet when the path crossed a small brook.

As soon as we'd unburdened ourselves from our packs and began to untie our laces, Dash spotted a suitcase lying half in, half out of the water. Curious, we walked over to it and lugged it out of the brook for inspection. The case was locked, but we opened it with little effort, as the lock was badly rusted. What we found inside was worth every blister, every ache we'd had,

Text Marking

Think about the setting and mood of the story.

☐	Box WHEN it takes place.
✗	Cross the box that shows WHEN the story is set.
☐	past
☐	present
☐	future
◯	Circle WHERE it takes place.
_____	Underline details that set the mood.

for it contained a treasure trove of valuable classic comics, collectors' items, all from the 1950s and 1960s. *Superman! Wonder Woman! Batman! Spider-Man! Green Lantern!* You name it, it was there. Some were partially waterlogged, but others were in pristine condition. We couldn't believe our good fortune.

We took a few issues to show the campers we were meeting, then we hid the case. Our plan was to return to it on our way back. Then we hiked onwards, feeling practically pain-free and eager to reach the campsite.

Name _____ Date _____

The Case

▶ **Answer each question. Give details from the discovery story.**

1 Who is telling the story?

▶ **A** Dash ▶ **B** a bear ▶ **C** a hiker ▶ **D** Batman

What helped you answer? _____

_____

_____

2 A **trove** (paragraph 3) is a _____.

▶ **A** trunk. ▶ **B** collection. ▶ **C** trail. ▶ **D** a wet pile.

What helped you answer? _____

_____

_____

3 Make an inference. How did the discovery affect the hikers?

_____

_____

_____

_____

_____

_____

4 Summarise the setting and mood of the story.

_____

_____

_____

_____

_____

_____

_____

_____

A World Away

Read the fantasy.
Then follow the instructions in the Text-Marking box.

The Kudans couldn't have been more excited as they left the vast car park, passed through security and entered the grounds of the newly opened 2019 World's Fair. Hallie, in particular, couldn't wait to see the newest advances in technology and engineering from around the world. With her parents' permission, she galloped ahead to the ticket booth.

Just as she was about to get in the queue, Hallie experienced an odd sensation, as if she'd passed through the silken mesh of a giant spiderweb. She tingled from head to toe, and felt a bit dizzy. After shaking her head and rubbing her eyes, she felt like herself again. Which exhibit should she direct the family to first? A guide dressed in wild-west clothing came to her rescue.

"I'd start at the nearby Palace of Electricity, young lady," he said, adding, "unless you'd rather brave the crowds to see the great Apache leader Geronimo in his tepee. Or maybe head to the main auditorium, where 24-year-old Helen Keller is giving a lecture. And Thomas Edison himself is at the Palace, demonstrating his new electrical socket."

Text Marking

Think about the key events in Hallie's experience.

◯ Circle at least five events in the story.

___ Underline details about each event.

Geronimo? Helen Keller? Edison? Those people are still alive? A signpost caught Hallie's eye. Its arrows pointed to the locations of a giant aviary, a wireless telegraph tower and a transportation building with horseless carriages. Beside the sign, a woman in a bonnet was selling freshly squeezed lemonade. *What's going on here? Where's the high-tech stuff?*

Fretting, Hallie raced back towards where she'd left her family. She thought she spotted them outside a tall gate so she ran through, not noticing the sign above. It read "Welcome to the World's Fair 1904!"

Name _____ Date _____

A World Away

▶ **Answer each question. Give details from the fantasy.**

1 Why did the guide suggest that Hallie visit the Palace of Electricity?

▶ **A** It was a palace.   ▶ **C** A famous inventor was there in person.

▶ **B** It had free snacks.   ▶ **D** It would be less scary than getting near an Apache warrior.

What helped you answer? _____

_____

_____

2 What does it mean to **brave the crowds** (paragraph 3)?

▶ **A** face them   ▶ **B** fear them   ▶ **C** save them   ▶ **D** avoid them

What helped you answer? _____

_____

_____

3 What about the fair puzzled Hallie?

_____

_____

_____

_____

_____

_____

4 Make an inference. What happened to Hallie?

_____

_____

_____

_____

_____

_____

_____

To Angkor Wat

Read the travel story.
Then follow the instructions in the Text-Marking box.

Solyna's grandparents were from Cambodia,

so she'd always hoped one day to visit the country

they left behind. She loved their stories of Angkor Wat,

a vast ancient city of temples and shrines about

the size of Manchester. Nearly overtaken by the jungle,

Angkor Wat was rediscovered and designated a World

Heritage Site in 1992.

   Two decades later, Solyna and her parents went

on a two-week tour of the land of her ancestors.

For Solyna, the trip's highlight would be the tour's

final destination: the many architectural, cultural and artistic

wonders of Angkor Wat. After spending the night in a nearby

town, the group left at 4am for Angkor Wat.

Text Marking

Think about the key events
of the travel story.

◯   Circle four main events.

_____   Underline details
about each event.

   An excursion starting so early and involving journeying

through the night-dark jungle unnerved the travellers as they

piled into the *tuk-tuks*. These motorcycles pulling open-air

trailers with bare benches were well-suited to the dusty trails

to Angkor Wat. Utter darkness and strange echoing sounds

enveloped them. Their friendly guide identified animal calls as

they approached the magnificent site. There they chose an open spot to await the sunrise.

   Solyna shivered before many pairs of eyes peering at her from the thick vines and bushes. She

nervously paced to stay calm, imagining the site appearing in the morning light. As the black sky became

grey, then streaked with orange, pink, purple and blue, the outlines of the majestic temples became visible.

With no other groups sharing their spot, the experience felt dreamlike. The gigantic but serene carved stone

faces of Angkor Wat seemed to beckon all tourists to explore their ageless secrets.

To Angkor Wat

▶ **Answer each question. Give details from the travel story.**

1 When did Solyna first learn about Angkor Wat?

▶ **A** from the World Heritage Site   ▶ **C** from family members

▶ **B** during her two-week tour   ▶ **D** from travel websites

What helped you answer? _____

_____

_____

2 Why did the tour group leave for Angkor Wat at such an early hour?

▶ **A** There is nothing in the story to explain this.

▶ **B** They wanted to get there in time to see the sunrise.

▶ **C** They wanted to hear the night sounds of the jungle.

▶ **D** They wanted to avoid traffic jams they might encounter.

What helped you answer? _____

_____

_____

3 Which event in the story do you think is most important? Explain.

_____

_____

_____

_____

_____

4 How does the author of the story build suspense and mood?

_____

_____

_____

_____

Name _____ Date _____

Before the Race

Read the sports story.

Then follow the instructions in the Text-Marking box.

The first thing Kelly did upon her arrival, the day before the big race, was to check into her hotel. Too excited to rest, she then took a short jog around the urban neighbourhood, trying to stay loose and relaxed. At the runners' dinner that night, she chatted with fellow entrants and wolfed down her fill of pasta and bread. After dinner, she retreated to her room for some peace and quiet and, she hoped, a solid night's rest.

But Kelly tossed and turned, too keyed up to sleep. She'd been training for this gruelling London Marathon for eight months. But she couldn't help worrying about injury or failure to finish the race. Eventually, she dozed off, though when her alarm rang at 5.00am, it seemed to her that she hadn't slept a wink. She arose anyway, yawned, stretched her leg muscles and yawned again. Then she ate breakfast and put on her running gear.

The shuttle bus taking runners to the starting line was packed, so she stood for the entire journey. Some runners were chatting in small groups. Others, like Kelly, kept silent,

Text Marking

Mark the sequence of events in the story.

☐   Box at least eight signal words about sequence and time.

_____ Underline key events in the hours before the race began.

imagining what the day's experience would be like. After half an hour, the bus arrived at the staging area, where she and the other marathoners picked up their numbers and pinned them on. Then Kelly, no longer sleepy, walked to where runners were congregating behind the starting line.

There, she did additional stretches while gazing over at the towers of the great bridge she'd soon be crossing. Beyond it, the city's dramatic skyline was brilliantly bathed in the morning sun. There was nearly an hour to go and she was eager and energised. When the race began at last, Kelly's heart pounded with excitement. Off she ran – only 42.4 kilometres to go!

Before the Race

▶ **Answer each question. Give details from the sports story.**

1 Which of the following is 42.4 kilometres long?

▶ **A** the bridge with the tall towers

▶ **C** the total length of the marathon course

▶ **B** the shuttle bus ride to the starting line

▶ **D** the distance from Kelly's home to the city

What helped you answer? _____

_____

_____

2 Which word or expression does not mean the same as **keyed up** (paragraph 2)?

▶ **A** jittery   ▶ **B** agitated   ▶ **C** worked up   ▶ **D** lonely

What helped you answer? _____

_____

_____

3 Make an inference. How would you characterise the process of preparing for a marathon?

_____

_____

_____

_____

_____

_____

4 Describe Kelly's emotions from the time she arrives in the city to when she starts running.

_____

_____

_____

_____

_____

_____

Name _____ Date _____

A Mini-Golf Gripe

Read the humorous story.
Then follow the instructions in the Text-Marking box.

"So, how was *your* day?"

The question caught me by surprise, for it's usually one of the green balls that engages me in conversation at the end of the day. But today, it was a yellow one that'd had a rough afternoon on the course and wanted some sympathy.

As assistant manager at Mulligan Mike's Mini-Golf, one of my jobs is to collect, clean and even comfort the hardworking golf balls. Today, this unhappy one sought my companionship.

"The morning was promising," the ball began, "as I was hidden under dozens of others in a bucket and hoped I might get the day off. That dream vanished around noon, when, to my dismay, the rowdiest little boy in a group fished me out. I knew full well the hazards that lay ahead, and I'm not just referring to the windmills, towers, tunnels and bridges.

"My troubles started right away. First, swinging the putter like a rounders bat, the youngster slammed away, causing me to leapfrog the boundaries of the first hole and land in the goldfish pond. One hole in and I was already soaking wet. Then I got dried off harshly and my misadventures began anew. Over the course of the next hour – a full year in golf-ball time – I got buried in sand, temporarily lost under a bush (where I tried to stay hidden), whacked again and again, and suffered bruise upon bruise. Lastly, he picked me up in his grimy little fingers and then, to complete my misery, bounced me HARD on the concrete path."

"Wow, you've had an agonising afternoon, golf ball, and I share your pain. Suppose I nestle you down deep into the ball bucket so you might get tomorrow off."

"Not exactly the answer I was seeking, Ralph," the ball glumly replied. "My greatest desire is to just retire."

Text Marking

Mark the sequence of events in the golf ball's retelling of its day.

☐ Box at least six signal words about sequence and time.

_____ Underline the key events in the ball's story.

A Mini-Golf Gripe

▶ **Answer each question. Give details from the humorous story.**

1 Why did the golf ball start a conversation with Ralph?

▶ **A** It wanted sympathy because of the rough day it had.

▶ **B** It wanted to be used on a real golf course.

▶ **C** It was wet and needed to be dried off.

▶ **D** It felt sorry for him.

What helped you answer? _____

_____

_____

2 How did the golf ball feel when the little boy chose it?

▶ **A** eager   ▶ **B** confused   ▶ **C** adventurous   ▶ **D** disheartened

What helped you answer? _____

_____

_____

3 What was Ralph's helpful suggestion for easing the yellow ball's discomfort and why did the ball react as it did?

_____

_____

_____

_____

_____

4 Make an inference. How would you describe the personality of the yellow golf ball?

_____

_____

_____

_____

Name _____ Date _____

The Gordian Knot

Read the myth.

Then follow the instructions in the Text-Marking box.

The ancient kingdom of Phrygia was located in what is now modern Turkey. During a time in its history, Phrygia found itself without a king. Lacking a strong ruler, the Phrygians feared for their safety. They prayed for guidance and consulted the oracle at Telmissus for advice. To their relief, the oracle declared that the next man to enter the city with an ox cart would become king.

Meanwhile, the peasant Gordius was driving his ox cart towards the Phrygian capital. As he travelled, a golden eagle landed on his cart, which Gordius interpreted as a good omen. Unable to determine its meaning, he continued his journey, trusting that the meaning would be revealed.

When Gordius entered the capital, the people greeted him with acclaim; the priests crowned him their new king. The capital of Phrygia was renamed Gordium. Now Gordius had a son, Midas, who stepped forwards to honour his father, to reassure the Phrygians and to pay homage to Zeus, king of all gods. He dedicated the ox cart to Zeus and tied it with an intricate knot. The knot was so complicated that whoever untied it would rule all of Asia, predicted the oracle. From then on, the knot was called the Gordian knot.

★ Text Marking ★

Identify two conflicts, or problems, in the story and how each gets solved.

☐	Box these signal words: **feared**, **prayed for guidance**, **relief**, **challengers** and **fulfilling the prophecy**
⬭	Circle each conflict or problem.
___	Underline each resolution.
C	Write C to indicate details about conflict.
R	Write R to indicate details about resolution.

As word spread about the knot and its promise, challengers arrived from everywhere to try to untie it. None succeeded. The Gordian knot held fast for generations until 333bce. That was when, according to legend, Alexander the Great came to Gordium, curious about the famed knot, which by now was weathered ever tighter. Unable to find its loose ends, Alexander dramatically cut the knot with a single stroke of his sword. He did go on to conquer much of Asia, thus fulfilling the prophecy.

The Gordian Knot

▶ **Answer each question. Give details from the myth.**

1 According to the myth, what is the purpose of an **oracle** (paragraph 1)?

▶ **A** to provide comfort   ▶ **C** to predict the future

▶ **B** to give good omens   ▶ **D** to pose riddles and puzzles

What helped you answer? _____

_____

_____

2 Nowadays, we describe a situation as a 'Gordian knot' if it is _____.

▶ **A** very old   ▶ **C** the way a leader is chosen

▶ **B** impossible to predict   ▶ **D** a demanding, complex problem

What helped you answer? _____

_____

_____

3 Alexander the Great was an actual historical figure who did conquer parts of Asia. How can a story be both mythical and real?

_____

_____

_____

_____

_____

4 Explain the connection between the peasant Gordius and the conqueror Alexander the Great.

_____

_____

_____

_____

_____

Name _____ Date _____

New Heights

Read the coming-of-age story.
Then follow the instructions in the Text-Marking box.

Marnie had always thought of herself as meek and fearful, as scared of her own shadow as she was of bats, spiders, snakes and barking dogs. Her lack of confidence became a greater problem as she approached Year 8. Somehow, she'd let herself be talked into embarking on an adventurous alpine backpacking trip.

When Marnie and her fears arrived at the 1.6 kilometre-high base camp, she knew, as did the others on the expedition, that many obstacles lay ahead. She was anxious, but vowed to take them on. She was prepared to learn how to trust herself.

On the website, Marnie read that experienced, supportive instructors would teach the group about camping, cooking in the wilderness, rock climbing and the necessity of teamwork. She knew she would learn to apply basic first aid, use a compass and read a map. Moreover, she understood full well that she and the others would be on their own, problem-solving and cooperating to reach assigned destinations in a rugged environment.

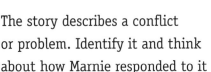

Text Marking

The story describes a conflict or problem. Identify it and think about how Marnie responded to it and overcame it.

☐   Box the conflict or problem.

⬭   Circle the ways Marnie reacted to the conflict.

___   Underline the resolution.

The terrain was rough indeed. While ascending to an altitude of 3000 metres, Marnie's team found themselves both on and off steep and rocky paths. She practised remaining calm and focused, which helped her apply what she'd learned. It surprised her how much confidence she gained with each completed task. She was learning deeper things, too – about herself. Marnie found her inner strength, which was now being tapped for the first time. She discovered that she could lead as well as follow, and she liked that feeling.

When she returned from the two-week challenge, Marnie felt proud of herself and invigorated. Sure, lightning, forest fires, mudslides and avalanches were still scary events, but Marnie was confident she could face them head on. She had developed new self-confidence and an eagerness to expand her horizons.

New Heights

▶ **Answer each question. Give details from the coming-of-age story.**

1 Who is telling the story?

▶ **A** a narrator   ▶ **B** an alpine instructor   ▶ **C** one of Marnie's teammates   ▶ **D** Marnie

What helped you answer? _____

_____

_____

2 Which was the most significant benefit of Marnie's trip?

▶ **A** She learned to read a compass.

▶ **B** She grew in self-confidence and inner strength.

▶ **C** She developed an ability to function at high altitudes.

▶ **D** She learned how to camp without harming the environment.

What helped you answer? _____

_____

_____

3 What inferences can you make about Marnie?

_____

_____

_____

_____

_____

4 A coming-of-age story explores a person's transition from childhood to maturity.
What features make this a coming-of-age story?

_____

_____

_____

_____

Name _____ Date _____

Clock Watching

Read the descriptive story.
Then follow the instructions in the Text-Marking box.

Many who pass through this immense, majestic train station take an occasional glance in my direction. I, meanwhile, have been observing them all for years from my bird's-eye perspective. I, you see, am an oversized clock perched high upon the wall.

At the moment, my hour hand is on the 10 and my minute hand is on the 12. That means the morning rush hour is winding down. But the concourse is still an obstacle course of scurrying people – some zig-zagging alone in the hall, others in pairs or groups. There's the usual assortment of commuters, looking purposeful or befuddled, harried or calm. They scoot past each other, not making eye contact, or bump into one another and apologise. They stop and chat. They assist one another by retrieving dropped papers or luggage. It's the same old bustling scene that plays out here every weekday.

Text Marking

Use context clues to unlock meaning.

○ Circle the words:
concourse, **befuddled**, **harried**, **bustling** and **gawkers**.

▭ Box the expression: **winding down**.

___ Underline context clues for each.

In a short while, the station will calm down enough for me to focus on what I really like watching – the entertainment. That's a part of life here that frequently *does* change. Of the collection of clowns, jugglers, musician and others that call this great hall their stage, my favourites are the people in costume. It warms my clock heart to see their plastic buckets fill with change.

I still fondly remember the guy dressed as Big Ben. His costume looked like the famed clock tower complete with chimes that rang on the hour. Sadly, he found another stage. This month's crowd favourite seems to be the Statue of Liberty, right now encircled by onlookers seemingly bewitched by every slight, silent tilt of her crowned, green head. Ah, but what's this I see – a newcomer? Yes, it's a dancing hot dog coated with mustard. This fellow is siphoning away some of the statue's gawkers. Maybe people are hungrier than they know. Oh, I love this station.

Clock Watching

▶ **Answer each question. Give details from the descriptive story.**

1 Which means about the same as **harried** (paragraph 2)?

▶ **A** funny   ▶ **B** frazzled   ▶ **C** casual   ▶ **D** relaxed

What helped you answer? _____

_____

_____

2 Which of the following is NOT an example of something **winding down** (paragraph 2)?

▶ **A** playing the second half of a football match   ▶ **C** being in the final week of school

▶ **B** having dessert at the end of a dinner   ▶ **D** sitting in the last carriage of a train

What helped you answer?_____

_____

_____

3 What makes this story quirky?

_____

_____

_____

_____

_____

_____

4 Suggest a possible location for the train station. Explain your choice.

_____

_____

_____

_____

_____

_____

_____

Name _____ Date _____

Bienvenue, Mr Lindbergh!

Read the historical fiction story.
Then follow the instructions in the Text-Marking box.

It was a good thing Marcelle's family had left early for the airfield, since the traffic jam was the worst Paris had ever seen. Thousands were gathering on that summer night in 1927, eager to witness history being made. Many car headlights remained on, ringing the grassy field with light, illuminating it for the brave pilot and his small, unstable plane. All eyes were on the night sky, and the buzz of excitement was palpable.

Charles Lindbergh circled the Eiffel Tower before making for the lit-up target north-east of the city. When, after more than 33 non-stop hours in the air, the bold aviator safely touched down at 10:22, he encountered a scene of instant pandemonium. Exultant people toppled a chain-link fence and raced across the field for a closer look at him and his *Spirit of St Louis*. Marcelle was among them.

"Wow," she exclaimed as she approached the monoplane. "Not only is it so tiny, all it's got is a cramped, one-seat cockpit and a single engine. Plus, it's covered only in fabric!"

"And look," her dad added, "there's no window in the front – he must've had to look out the side to see where he was going!"

> ### Text Marking
>
> Use context clues to unlock meaning.
>
> ⬭ Circle the words:
> **illuminating, palpable, pandemonium, exultant** and **thronged.**
>
> ☐ Box the expression:
> **caught her eye.**
>
> ___ Underline context clues for each.

While the family investigated the plane and others swarmed over it, grabbing what they could as souvenirs, hundreds of others thronged around the startled Lindbergh. The exhausted hero seemed overwhelmed as they carried him off the field, tugging at his coat and yanking at his leather helmet. Marcelle swore she spotted the famous dancer Isadora Duncan among them, caught her eye and earned a smile.

When Marcelle finally got back home, she couldn't sleep, for witnessing the conclusion of the first transatlantic flight was the experience of a lifetime. But she didn't mind; Lindbergh hadn't slept either.

Name _____ Date _____

Bienvenue, Mr Lindbergh!

▶ **Answer each question. Give details from the story.**

1 You would probably feel **exultant** (paragraph 2) if you...

▶ **A** won a championship trophy.   ▶ **C** didn't get enough sleep.

▶ **B** ate a particularly big meal.   ▶ **D** got a job babysitting.

What helped you answer? _____

_____

_____

2 When something is **palpable** (paragraph 1), it is quite...

▶ **A** loud.   ▶ **B** startling.   ▶ **C.** excitable.   ▶ **D** noticeable.

What helped you answer? _____

_____

_____

3 Describe some elements of a scene of **pandemonium** (paragraph 2).

_____

_____

_____

_____

_____

4 Make inferences. What details in the story support that Lindbergh's flight was a historic and heroic accomplishment?

_____

_____

_____

_____

_____

_____

_____

Name _____ Date _____

Under Review

Read the food story.

Then follow the instructions in the Text-Marking box.

Hunter and Kiki frequently post reviews of restaurants they go to. One day recently, each posted a review of the same restaurant on their favourite dining site, YUMM.com.

Hunter wrote this review:

It was bad enough that Manuela's was terribly crowded and deafening, but the wretched food and second-rate service irked us all. Since we could hardly hear what one another was saying, we all focused on our food, which proved to be a disappointing decision.

I started with the fish taco, a bone-dry and tasteless concoction through and through. Undaunted and trying to remain optimistic, I then bit into a chicken enchilada, the speciality of the house. In contrast, this dish was mouth-watering. But the flan I had for dessert, which should've been creamy and sweet, was lumpy and dull. I don't know what the others thought of their meals because I couldn't hear them above the racket.

In summation, I would rate this eatery 1½ Yumms. Still, if you prefer appalling food at steep prices, this may be the place for you.

And Kiki wrote this:

If you don't mind liveliness and waiting a bit for service, run, don't walk, to Manuela's Restaurant. You won't be disappointed; the ambience is welcoming and the prices won't give you indigestion.

As opposed to what another reviewer has written, my fish taco was a truly memorable dish, flavoursome and succulent, a wonderful way to start a meal. The other starters our group ordered were scrumptious, too. And aside from the chicken enchilada, which was as miniscule in taste as it was colossal in size, the other main courses pleased all diners. And, oh that flan was heavenly – creamy, sweet, and fit for a king. I gladly give this place 3 Yumms, and can't wait to return.

Text Marking

Compare and contrast the two reviews.

☐ Box signal words for comparing and contrasting.

◯ Circle the ways the reviews are the same.

___ Underline the ways they are different.

■ **SCHOLASTIC**

Name _____ Date _____

Under Review

▶ **Answer each question. Give details from the food story.**

1 If you are **undaunted** (paragraph 4), you are...

▶ **A** appalled. ▶ **B** focused. ▶ **C** courageous. ▶ **D** scared off.

What helped you answer? _____

_____

_____

2 Which of the following is something both reviewers agreed upon?

▶ **A** the poor service ▶ **B** the flan ▶ **C** the prices ▶ **D** the fish taco

What helped you answer? _____

_____

_____

3 Summarise how the two reviews are connected.

_____

_____

_____

_____

_____

_____

_____

_____

4 How can you explain the vast differences in the two reviews?

_____

_____

_____

_____

_____

_____

Name _____ Date _____

Theatres New and Old

Read the theatre story.

Then follow the instructions in the Text-Marking box.

Like his classmates, Zack was eager for the show to begin. They sat in the Milton Keynes Theatre, there to see *The Frogs*, a play by the Greek playwright Aristophanes. Inside the theatre, most of the comfortable seats were filled; the room was abuzz. The large, modern theatre, which opened in 1999, was colourful and welcoming. Compared to the storm raging outside, it was cosy.

On the same April day, Zack's aunt Viola was 3400 kilometres away exploring the ancient outdoor theatre at Epidaurus, Greece. That symmetrical stone venue, built nearly 2400 years ago, was carved into a natural hillside, where warm spring breezes rustled the leaves of trees that formed a living backdrop. This amphitheatre, which can accommodate over 12,000 visitors on its hard stone benches, is still used for plays and events. However, no play was being performed that day.

Back in Milton Keynes, an announcer asked everyone to turn off all electronic devices as the house lights dimmed. Actors quietly entered to take their places. Zack took a last glance at his programme and focused on the stage.

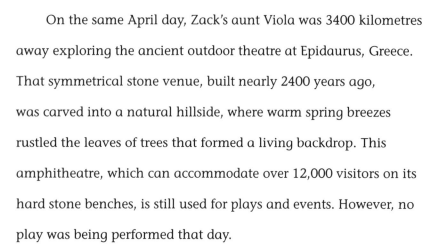

Text Marking

Compare and contrast the two theatre venues.

☐ Box signal words for comparing and contrasting.

◯ Circle ways the venues are alike.

___ Underline ways they are different.

The simple theatre at Epidaurus had no programmes, no speaker system and no house lights – just daylight. Its most remarkable feature was its near-perfect natural acoustics. Viola's tour guide stood on stage and spoke to visitors 30 rows away. Everyone could make out every word. By contrast, actors in Milton Keynes wore body microphones to amplify their voices.

Zack enjoyed the centuries-old play performed in the Buckinghamshire venue. Meanwhile, his aunt appreciated a centuries-old Greek venue with her tour guide as the sole performer, with perhaps a chorus of ghosts for atmosphere.

Name _____ Date _____

Theatres New and Old

▶ **Answer each question. Give details from the theatre story.**

1 Who wrote the play that Zack's class went to see?

▶ **A** Milton Keynes   ▶ **B** Viola   ▶ **C** Aristophanes   ▶ **D** Epidaurus

What helped you answer? _____

_____

_____

2 Why do you think that the room was **abuzz** at the Milton Keynes theatre (paragraph 1)?

▶ **A** The audience was excited to see the play.

▶ **B** An annoying noise was coming from the speakers.

▶ **C** There were bees in the audience.

▶ **D** The acoustics were so clear that the audience could hear everything.

What helped you answer? _____

_____

_____

3 Summarise the key ways that an amphitheatre differs from a theatre like the Milton Keynes theatre.

_____

_____

_____

_____

4 Does Aunt Viola see a real play? What does 'his aunt appreciated a centuries-old Greek venue with her tour guide as the sole performer, with perhaps a chorus of ghosts for atmosphere' mean?

_____

_____

_____

_____

Name _____ Date _____

What, No TV?

Read the family story.
Then follow the instructions in the Text-Marking box.

When Enid and Gary got the news, they bubbled with excitement. Not everyone, they understood, gets to live in a real medieval castle. But they were about to. That's because their parents, both historians, volunteered to be the castle's caretakers for a year. The only bad part was really bad. They'd be so far from their friends.

As Maid Enid and Squire Gary began reading about castles, their eagerness to begin their stay grew. And when they stood for the first time before the towering, 800-year-old stone castle, replete with impenetrable walls, slits for windows and crenelated towers, their anticipation rose to new heights. They exuberantly crossed the drawbridge into their new home.

The first few days brought glorious hours of exploring its great rooms and halls, its dark dungeons and imposing towers. But after a week, the fun began to dissipate in the face of the

---

Text Marking

Make an inference: What can you say about this family?

_____ Underline text clues.

 Think about what you already know.

---

realities of castle life. The massive stone walls and remote location severely limited the reception for their electronic devices: no texting for a year. Plus, there was no TV. And despite fireplaces large enough to stand in, the rooms were dimly lit, damp and often cold. Besides being so 'middle-aged' and uncomfortable, the castle was enormous. When Benny the beagle scampered off, it took hours of searching every nook, stairway and secret passage to find him.

But the family survived their unusual year, keeping busy with the many tasks of daily living without electricity and running water. They also learned to gather firewood and build fires, pump water and prepare and preserve food. They found entertainment in playing games, telling stories and making music. Still, when their parents next considered a year on an icebreaker in the Arctic, first mates Enid and Gary got cold feet.

What, No TV?

▶ **Answer each question. Give details from the family story.**

1 Which best describes Enid and Gary's parents, based on the choices they make?

▶ **A** They are adventurous.   ▶ **C** They are fearful.

▶ **B** They are middle-aged.   ▶ **D** They like the cold and damp.

What helped you answer? _____

_____

_____

2 Which choice means about the same as **impenetrable** (paragraph 2)?

▶ **A** stony   ▶ **B** densely solid   ▶ **C** medieval   ▶ **D** towering

What helped you answer? _____

_____

_____

3 Make an inference. Why might Enid and Gary be less excited about living on an icebreaker than in a castle?

_____

_____

_____

_____

_____

4 A cautionary tale is a story that gives a warning. In what way is this story a cautionary tale?

_____

_____

_____

_____

_____

Name _____ Date _____

Bad Break

Read the realistic fiction story.
Then follow the instructions in the Text-Marking box.

Ursula, a good student and talented artist, planned to attend art school to improve her skills. But her summer plans were in jeopardy when, walking her dog in May, she tripped over the lead, landed badly and broke her right leg. The moulded plaster cast Ursula wore home from the hospital immobilised her leg from knee to ankle. She'd wear it for eight weeks while finishing the school year.

Ursula returned to school a few days later using crutches. She was strong, but found that navigating busy corridors and the canteen proved more awkward than she'd expected. Like any child would be, Ursula was uncomfortable with this new reality. Although classmates freely offered to carry her books, bring things for her and help her get in and out of chairs, she always resisted, insisting, "No thanks, I'm fine." Embarrassed to feel weak and needy, she rejected help whenever it was offered.

> ## Text Marking
>
> Make an inference: How does the story reveal Ursula's personality?
>
> _____ Underline text clues.
>
> Think about what you already know.

Things changed one day in art class, where students were collaborating to paint a mural. The project demanded sharing equipment and lots of bending and reaching. Fretting that she'd feel useless, maybe even mess up the mural, Ursula asked Mr Wells to excuse her to sketch by herself at her desk. "You have lessons to learn right here, Ursula," the teacher gently suggested.

"What can I learn from messing everything up?" she asked sharply.

"You could learn to let others help you," replied Mr Wells. "There's no shame in needing help. We all want to support you, and you should learn to accept kindness." With the sweep of his arm, Mr Wells accidentally knocked a clipboard off his desk. Ursula reached out with her crutch and gently nudged it towards him. Mr Wells smiled. Ursula, experiencing an *Aha!* moment, smiled back.

SCHOLASTIC

Name _____ Date _____

Bad Break

▶ **Answer each question. Give details from the realistic fiction story.**

1 How does Ursula show that she is **uncomfortable with this new reality** (paragraph 2)?

▶ **A** She asks her teacher for help.   ▶ **C** She refuses help, though she struggles to get around.

▶ **B** She reads a lot.   ▶ **D** She eats lots of sweets.

What helped you answer? _____

_____

_____

2 What theme does the author explore in this story?

▶ **A** loyalty   ▶ **B** avoiding danger   ▶ **C** expressing pity   ▶ **D** adapting to change

What helped you answer? _____

_____

_____

3 Make an inference. Why do you think Ursula spoke to her teacher so sharply?

_____

_____

_____

_____

_____

_____

_____

4 How would you explain Ursula's *Aha!* moment at the end of the story?

_____

_____

_____

_____

_____

Name _____ Date _____

Musical Finale

Read the music story.
Then follow the instructions in the Text-Marking box.

Alyssa Linton had always been a musical child. Her mother bragged that her daughter sang before she spoke, that she picked out melodies on the family piano before she ever took lessons. So it made sense that Alyssa cultivated that early fascination for anything she could use to make music. Her voice was her first instrument. Then came piano, recorder and accordion. She hoped to begin guitar lessons to expand her musical capabilities.

One June, the Linton family organised a reunion for relatives from around the country. Nearly seventy people came, representing five generations! On the reunion's last evening, everyone gathered in the party room of a local restaurant for a festive farewell dinner. People wearing name tags were seated at round tables, where laughter and conversation flowed easily. Alyssa sat at a table with children mostly her age. Though the talk was lively and friendly, Alyssa got distracted by the many water glasses near her.

★ Text Marking ★

Summarise the story.

◯ Circle the main idea.

_____ Underline important details.

On a whim, she tapped hers with a spoon and noticed that it rang out with a clear, pleasing tone. She began asking people to lend her their water glasses so she could entertain the whole table. Puzzled, relatives sipped some water and passed their glasses to Alyssa.

One by one, Alyssa adjusted the amount of water in each glass to create a musical scale of twelve distinct notes. Once she'd tuned and arranged the glasses, Alyssa began playing melodies by tapping them. The others at the table stopped talking to listen with delight, soon requesting tunes for Alyssa to try. In no time, she was tapping with two spoons to play melody and harmony!

Before long, relatives at other tables started making their own water-glass instruments. Within moments, the room sounded like a carnival with people of all ages singing, playing, clapping and dancing!

Name _____ Date _____

Musical Finale

▶ **Answer each question. Give details from the music story.**

1 Which best describes the theme of this story?

▶ **A** family values   ▶ **B** joy of music   ▶ **C** generations   ▶ **D** carnival

What helped you answer? _____

_____

_____

2 Which of the following instruments is most like the instrument Alyssa created?

▶ **A** accordion   ▶ **B.** guitar   ▶ **C** tambourine   ▶ **D** xylophone

What helped you answer? _____

_____

_____

3 Make an inference. Why do you think the many water glasses distracted Alyssa at the party?

_____

_____

_____

_____

_____

_____

_____

4 Summarise how Alyssa affected the family farewell party.

_____

_____

_____

_____

_____

_____

Name _____   Date _____

Caving

Read the adventure story.
Then follow the instructions in the Text-Marking box.

Have you ever had an experience that was unnerving while it was happening, but when speaking of it later on, you retell it as a wonderful adventure? My friends and I did when we took a guided tour of a lava tube at the base of an extinct volcano.

"Listen carefully!" said Dan, our guide. "A lava tube is a cave formed by flowing lava that has hardened and cooled. Some of these natural underground conduits are long and large enough for caving. But others can be cramped and difficult to enter and explore, like parts of this one. But I see that you've got good hiking shoes and bright torches, so let's go!"

We giggled, gulped and followed Dan down into the darkness. After clambering down between sharp stalagmites and ducking under the perilous, icicle-like stalactites, we reached a room-sized chamber. It was smooth underfoot and walking was easier. Side tubes beckoned, so Dan led us into one, cautioning, "Slow and steady, cavers."

Text Marking

Summarise the story.
Think about its theme.

◯ Circle the main idea of the story.

_____ Underline important details.

This tunnel quickly narrowed until we found ourselves crawling and squirming, getting scratched in the process. Despite Dan's confident assertion that all was well, we felt scared. So, we were relieved when he recognised that wriggling wasn't our thing, and led us back to the main chamber. It was slow-going, and what was creepy about it got even creepier when we heard a rustling sound behind us. "Just a bat," Dan advised. Nonetheless, that sound got us and our scraped knees scrambling out as fast as we could.

When I tell this caving story today, I speak of it as a thrilling escapade, fun from beginning to end. In fact, despite the presence of a qualified guide, we were all nervous, and never happier to be safely above ground.

Caving

▶ **Answer each question. Give details from the adventure story.**

1 **Conduits** (paragraph 2) are...

▶ **A** adventures. ▶ **C** explorers.

▶ **B** tubes. ▶ **D** rivers.

What helped you answer? _____

_____

_____

2 What do you call the formations that hang from the ceilings of some caves?

▶ **A** bats ▶ **B** side tubes ▶ **C** stalagmites ▶ **D** stalactites

What helped you answer? _____

_____

_____

3 Summarise how the details in paragraphs 2–5 support the point the author makes in the first paragraph.

_____

_____

_____

_____

_____

_____

4 Make an inference. Why does the narrator mention that the hikers giggled and gulped as they entered the lava tube?

_____

_____

_____

_____

_____

Answers

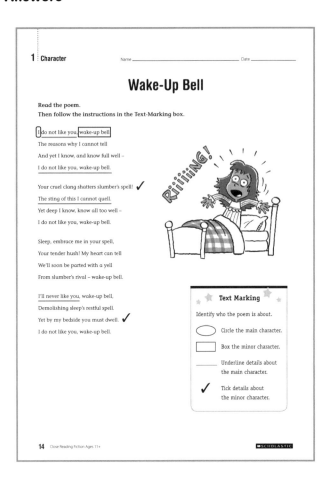

◀ **Sample Text Markings**

Passage 1: Wake-Up Bell

1 B; *Sample answer:* I picked B because I could tell that the bell is by the bedside, so it must be an alarm clock.

2 C; *Sample answer:* I picked C because the poem blames the wake-up bell for ruining the speaker's sleep, so a rival must be a challenger to the peace of sleeping.

3 *Sample answer:* The poem is written in the first person (clues: 'I', 'me', 'my'). The speaker doesn't like the wake-up bell, will never like it and describes it as a heartless brute.

4 *Sample answer:* The central idea is that the speaker hates waking up from a restful sleep to the unwelcome clang of an alarm clock, though it seems she must do this on a regular basis.

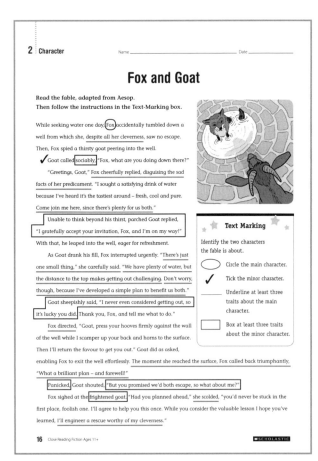

◀ **Sample Text Markings**

Passage 2: Fox and Goat

1 D; *Sample answer:* I picked D because I think it means that Goat is so thirsty that, instead of taking a moment to think of possible results of jumping into a well, he just jumps.

2 B; *Sample answer:* I picked B because it seems to best summarise the error Goat made by failing to think ahead.

3 *Sample answer:* Fox is clever, resourceful, lies easily and enjoys gloating. She tricked Goat into coming down into the well to provide her with a means of escape, but had no intention of returning the favour. Still, she kept her promise this time.

4 *Sample answer:* It reminds me of someone giving in to a dare to avoid seeming weak, but ending up in even more trouble because of failing to think ahead about what would most likely happen.

◀ **Sample Text Markings**

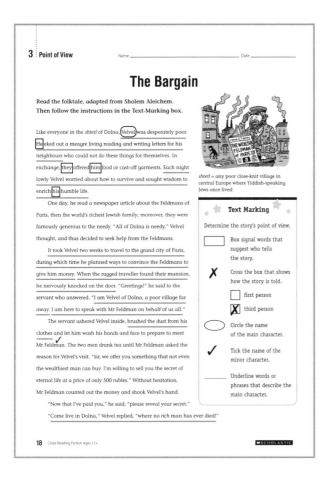

Passage 3: The Bargain

1 C; *Sample answer:* I picked C because the story says that the Feldmans were the world's richest Jewish family.

2 D; *Sample answer:* I picked D because the other three words relate to poverty and lack of possessions, but 'eternal' means lasting forever.

3 *Sample answer:* Velvel is very poor but hard-working. He is bold to travel a great distance to ask a wealthy man for help. Finally, he is clever. His 'secret' of eternal life isn't exactly a lie; Velvel uses this sad truth to get Feldman to give him money.

4 *Sample answer:* According to the folktale, the Feldmans were wealthy and generous to the poor. So maybe Mr Feldman paid Velvel to respect his courage in coming to ask, and to show understanding of the difficulties of poverty. Also, 500 rubles was probably a trivial amount of money to Mr Feldman, but worth far more to Velvel. And, since Feldman was very wealthy, the only thing he DIDN'T have was eternal life.

◀ **Sample Text Markings**

Passage 4: Becoming B-boys

1 B; *Sample answer:* I picked B because A and C make sense with the topic, and D could make sense as a boastful name, but B is the least likely.

2 D; *Sample answer:* I picked D because I understood that learning hip-hop dance would be difficult and might be slow at first. I think Cato was preparing the b-boys for hard work.

3 *Sample answer:* The author uses the first person point of view to give readers an inside view of how someone can learn hip-hop dancing. Because the story is told by the person learning, readers can follow his development.

4 *Sample answer:* The narrator and his crew wanted to learn this skill, but may have underestimated its difficulty. But they stuck with it, practised hard and improved to the point of wanting to perform in public.

Answers

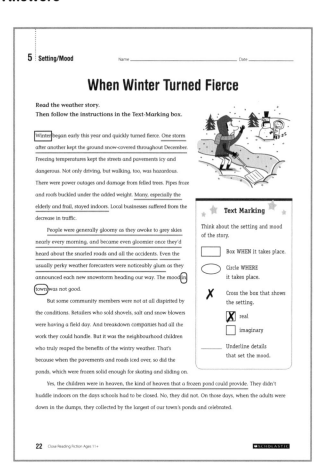

Passage 5: When Winter Turned Fierce

1 C; *Sample answer:* I picked C because it is the answer that best fits the story, explaining that many were unhappy, but not everyone.

2 D; *Sample answer:* I picked D because I worked out that 'dispirited' means unhappy or disappointed.

3 *Sample answer:* I think that weather affects people in different ways. Weather that might be awful for some, and make them unhappy, could be beneficial for others and make those people glad.

4 *Sample answer:* I think the author lists things like icy roads, frozen pipes, fallen trees and buckling roofs to show people who may not live in cold climates what damage so much snow can do.

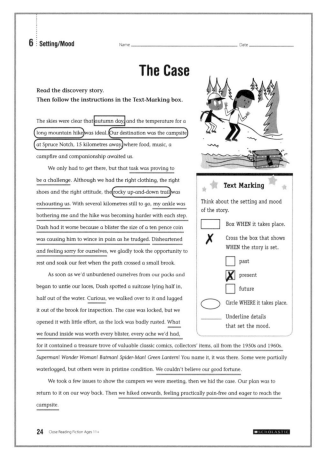

Passage 6: The Case

1 C; *Sample answer:* I picked C because the person hiking with Dash is the one describing their moods during the hike and the discovery.

2 B; *Sample answer:* I picked B because the hikers found a collection of comics, which are described as 'collectors' items'. Also, I know the expression 'treasure trove' to mean a collection of valuables, like gold and silver objects.

3 *Sample answer:* The hikers, previously very tired, became giddy once they found the valuable comics. Their discovery made it easier for them to ignore their discomforts and continue their trek.

4 *Sample answer:* The story is set along a mountain trail in autumn. The hikers become miserable due to exhaustion and physical discomfort. Their glum mood changes upon unexpectedly coming across a valuable collection of old comic books.

A World Away

Read the fantasy.
Then follow the instructions in the Text-Marking box.

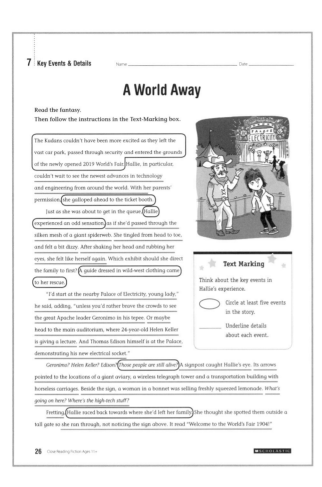

The Kudans couldn't have been more excited as they left the vast car park, passed through security and entered the grounds of the newly opened 2019 World's Fair. Hallie, in particular, couldn't wait to see the newest advances in technology and engineering from around the world. With her parents' permission, she galloped ahead to the ticket booth.

Just as she was about to get in the queue, Hallie experienced an odd sensation, as if she'd passed through the silken mesh of a giant spiderweb. She tingled from head to toe, and felt a bit dizzy. After shaking her head and rubbing her eyes, she felt like herself again. Which exhibit should she direct the family to first? A guide dressed in wild-west clothing came to her rescue.

"I'd start at the nearby Palace of Electricity, young lady," he said, adding, "unless you'd rather brave the crowds to see the great Apache leader Geronimo in his tepee. Or maybe head to the main auditorium, where 24-year-old Helen Keller is giving a lecture. And Thomas Edison himself is at the Palace, demonstrating his new electrical socket."

Geronimo? Helen Keller? Edison? Those people are still alive? A signpost caught Hallie's eye. Its arrows pointed to the locations of a giant aviary, a wireless telegraph tower and a transportation building with horseless carriages. Beside the sign, a woman in a bonnet was selling freshly squeezed lemonade. *What's going on here? Where's the high-tech stuff?*

Fretting, Hallie raced back towards where she'd left her family. She thought she spotted them outside a tall gate so she ran through, not noticing the sign above. It read "Welcome to the World's Fair 1904!"

Text Marking

Think about the key events in Hallie's experience.

◯ Circle at least five events in the story.

___ Underline details about each event.

◀ **Sample Text Markings**

Passage 7: A World Away

1 C; *Sample answer:* I picked C because in the third paragraph, the guide mentions that Thomas Edison himself would be there.

2 A; *Sample answer:* I picked A because I think the guide was telling Hallie that many people would be trying to see Geronimo and she might have to wait a long time.

3 *Sample answer:* I think she was puzzled by the exhibits, which featured people she knew were no longer alive and inventions that had first appeared long ago.

4 *Sample answer:* I think something made her time-travel back to the 1904 fair, where she saw exhibits that were very advanced and modern back then, but old-fashioned to her modern mind.

To Angkor Wat

Read the travel story.
Then follow the instructions in the Text-Marking box.

Solyna's grandparents were from Cambodia, so she'd always hoped one day to visit the country they left behind. She loved their stories of Angkor Wat, a vast ancient city of temples and shrines about the size of Manchester. Nearly overtaken by the jungle, Angkor Wat was rediscovered and designated a World Heritage Site in 1992.

Two decades later, Solyna and her parents went on a two-week tour of the land of her ancestors. For Solyna, the trip's highlight would be the tour's final destination: the many architectural, cultural and artistic wonders of Angkor Wat. After spending the night in a nearby town, the group left at 4am for Angkor Wat.

An excursion starting so early and involving journeying through the night-dark jungle unnerved the travellers as they piled into the *tuk-tuks*. These motorcycles pulling open-air trailers with bare benches were well-suited to the dusty trails to Angkor Wat. Utter darkness and strange echoing sounds enveloped them. Their friendly guide identified animal calls as they approached the magnificent site. There they chose an open spot to await the sunrise.

Solyna shivered before many pairs of eyes peering at her from the thick vines and bushes. She nervously paced to stay calm, imagining the site appearing in the morning light. As the black sky became grey, then streaked with orange, pink, purple and blue, the outlines of the majestic temples became visible. With no other groups sharing their spot, the experience felt dreamlike. The gigantic but serene carved stone faces of Angkor Wat seemed to beckon all tourists to explore their ageless secrets.

Text Marking

Think about the key events of the travel story.

◯ Circle four main events.

___ Underline details about each event.

◀ **Sample Text Markings**

Passage 8: To Angkor Wat

1 C; *Sample answer:* I picked C because it says in the first paragraph that Solyna's grandparents told her stories about Angkor Wat, which interested her.

2 B; *Sample answer:* I picked B because the events of the story helped me understand that the tourists wanted to experience Angkor Wat in the stillness of a beautiful sunrise.

3 *Sample answer:* I think the most important event is Solyna and her parents taking the two-week tour to Cambodia. That's the reason for the story and it explains all the other events and details.

4 *Sample answer:* The author begins with facts to set the scene and make a family connection to build interest for Solyna's trip. The many descriptive and sensory details help readers imagine how it might feel for Solyna and other tourists. The illustration of the stone faces reinforces the amazing features of Angkor Wat.

Answers

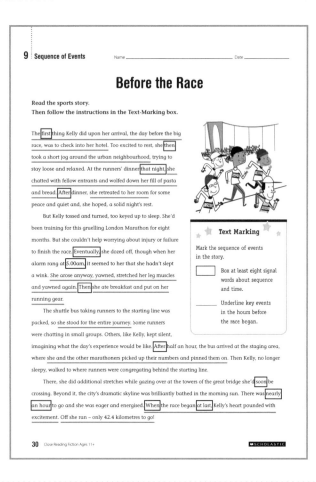
◀ **Sample Text Markings**

Passage 9: Before the Race

1 C; *Sample answer:* I picked C because I understood that, in the last sentence, '42.4 kilometres to go' refers to the length of the difficult race.

2 D; *Sample answer:* I picked D because all the other choices mean about the same as 'keyed up' or 'excited'.

3 *Sample answer:* I think it must be a thrilling and demanding experience that begins well before the race itself and has many parts. Like other dedicated runners, Kelly went through a lot to be ready for the race.

4 *Sample answer:* Kelly is filled with anticipation; she seeks peace and quiet to prepare for the race, but has a hard time sleeping, worried about how she will do. By the time she reaches the starting line, she is excited, energised and eager to begin.

◀ **Sample Text Markings**

Passage 10: A Mini-Golf Gripe

1 A; *Sample answer:* I picked A because that's what Ralph said the ball wanted.

2 D; *Sample answer:* I picked D because the ball said it was dismayed and I can tell from context clues that 'dismayed' means the same as 'disheartened'.

3 *Sample answer:* Ralph suggested placing the ball deep down in the ball bucket so that no one would choose it the next day. The ball would much rather retire from the game for good.

4 *Sample answer:* I think the ball is a complainer with strong views that feels sorry for itself, but that it is clever and has a gentle sense of humour. And I think it likes to talk a lot.

The Gordian Knot

Read the myth.
Then follow the instructions in the Text-Marking box.

The ancient kingdom of Phrygia was located in what is now modern Turkey. During a time in its history, Phrygia found itself **(C)** without a king. Lacking a strong ruler, the Phrygians feared for their safety. They prayed for guidance and consulted the oracle at Telmissus for advice. To their relief, the oracle declared that the next man to enter the city with an ox cart would become king.

Meanwhile, the peasant Gordius was driving his ox cart towards the Phrygian capital. As he travelled, a golden eagle landed on his cart, which Gordius interpreted as a good omen. Unable to determine its meaning, he continued his journey, trusting that the meaning would be revealed.

(R) When Gordius entered the capital, the people greeted him with acclaim; the priests crowned him their new king. The capital of Phrygia was renamed Gordium. Now Gordius had a son, Midas, who stepped forwards to honour his father, **(R)** to reassure the Phrygians and to pay homage to Zeus, king of all gods. He dedicated the ox cart to Zeus and tied it with an intricate knot. The knot was so complicated that whoever untied it would rule all of Asia, predicted the oracle. From then on, the knot was called the Gordian knot.

(C) As word spread about the knot and its promise, challengers arrived from everywhere to try to untie it. None succeeded. The Gordian knot held fast for generations until 333BCE. That was when, according to legend, Alexander the Great came to Gordium, curious about the famed knot, which by now was weathered ever tighter. Unable to find its loose ends, Alexander dramatically cut the knot with a single stroke of his **(R)** sword. He did go on to conquer much of Asia, thus fulfilling the prophecy.

Text Marking

Identify two conflicts, or problems, in the story and how each gets solved.

▢ Box these signal words: **feared, prayed for guidance, relief, challengers** and **fulfilling the prophecy**

◯ Circle each conflict or problem.

___ Underline each resolution.

C Write C to indicate details about conflict.

R Write R to indicate details about resolution.

◀ Sample Text Markings

Passage 11: The Gordian Knot

1 C; *Sample answer:* I picked C because this is exactly what the oracle at Telmissus did – both for Gordius to become king and for whoever solved the Gordian knot to rule Asia.

2 D; *Sample answer:* I picked D because the myth says again and again how difficult it was to untie the knot, and most people who tried failed. So today, a 'Gordian knot' is an extremely challenging problem.

3 *Sample answer:* The mythical part is the prediction by the oracle that whoever untied the Gordian knot would rule Asia. It's mythical that a knot could have such powers. The myth provides a heroic explanation for Alexander's actual feats.

4 *Sample answer:* The oracle foresaw that Gordius would be the new king of Phrygia. His rise was honoured by Midas, who dedicated the ox cart and tied the Gordian knot. Much later, Alexander the Great supposedly defeated the Gordian knot, thus ensuring his success as a conqueror.

New Heights

Read the coming-of-age story.
Then follow the instructions in the Text-Marking box.

Marnie had always thought of herself as meek and fearful, as scared of her own shadow as she was of bats, spiders, snakes and barking dogs. Her lack of confidence became a greater problem as she approached Year 8. Somehow, she'd let herself be talked into embarking on an adventurous alpine backpacking trip.

When Marnie and her fears arrived at the 1.6 kilometre-high base camp, she knew, as did the others on the expedition, that many obstacles lay ahead. She was anxious, but vowed to take them on. She was prepared to learn how to trust herself.

On the website, Marnie read that experienced, supportive instructors would teach the group about camping, cooking in the wilderness, rock climbing and the necessity of teamwork. She knew she would learn to apply basic first aid, use a compass and read a map. Moreover, she understood full well that she and the others would be on their own, problem-solving and cooperating to reach assigned destinations in a rugged environment.

The terrain was rough indeed. While ascending to an altitude of 3000 metres, Marnie's team found themselves both on and off steep and rocky paths. She practised remaining calm and focused, which helped her apply what she'd learned. It surprised her how much confidence she gained with each completed task. She was learning deeper things, too – about herself. Marnie found her inner strength, which was now being tapped for the first time. She discovered that she could lead as well as follow, and she liked that feeling.

When she returned from the two-week challenge, Marnie felt proud of herself and invigorated. Sure, lightning, forest fires, mudslides and avalanches were still scary events, but Marnie was confident she could face them head on. She had developed new self-confidence and an eagerness to expand her horizons.

Text Marking

The story describes a conflict or problem. Identify it and think about how Marnie responded to it and overcame it.

▢ Box the conflict or problem.

◯ Circle the ways Marnie reacted to the conflict.

___ Underline the resolution.

◀ Sample Text Markings

Passage 12: New Heights

1 A; *Sample answer:* I picked A because none of the other choices is supported by the text.

2 B; *Sample answer:* While Marnie benefited from all four choices, it was B that I think is most significant to her.

3 *Sample answer:* Although Marnie was afraid of things and lacked confidence, I think she was braver than she realised. She was bold enough to agree to take this challenging trip and strong enough to succeed and learn from it.

4 *Sample answer:* In a coming-of-age story, a character learns to overcome something and, as a result, becomes more mature. Marnie grew up thanks to the challenges she faced and met on the backpacking trip.

Answers

◀ **Sample Text Markings**

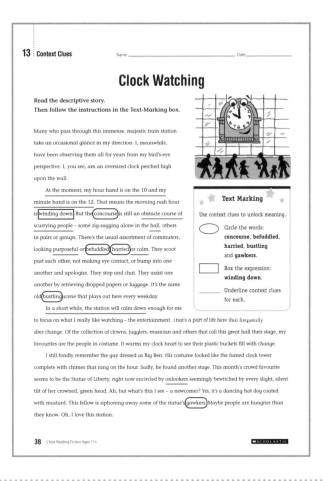

Clock Watching

Read the descriptive story.
Then follow the instructions in the Text-Marking box.

Many who pass through this immense, majestic train station take an occasional glance in my direction. I, meanwhile, have been observing them all for years from my bird's-eye perspective. I, you see, am an oversized clock perched high upon the wall.

At the moment, my hour hand is on the 10 and my minute hand is on the 12. That means the morning rush hour is winding down. But the concourse is still an obstacle course of scurrying people – some zig-zagging alone in the hall, others in pairs or groups. There's the usual assortment of commuters, looking purposeful or befuddled, harried or calm. They scoot past each other, not making eye contact, or bump into one another and apologise. They stop and chat. They assist one another by retrieving dropped papers or luggage. It's the same old bustling scene that plays out here every weekday.

In a short while, the station will calm down enough for me to focus on what I really like watching – the entertainment. That's a part of life that frequently does change. Of the collection of clowns, jugglers, musician and others that call this great hall their stage, my favourites are the people in costume. It warms my clock heart to see their plastic buckets fill with change.

I still fondly remember the guy dressed as Big Ben. His costume looked like the famed clock tower complete with chimes that rang on the hour. Sadly, he found another stage. This month's crowd favourite seems to be the Statue of Liberty, right now encircled by onlookers seemingly bewitched by every slight, silent tilt of her crowned, green head. Ah, but what's this I see – a newcomer? Yes, it's a dancing hot dog coated with mustard. This fellow is siphoning away some of the statue's gawkers. Maybe people are hungrier than they know. Oh, I love this station.

Text Marking

Use context clues to unlock meaning.

○ Circle the words:
concourse, befuddled, harried, bustling and **gawkers.**

▭ Box the expression:
winding down.

___ Underline context clues for each.

◀ **Sample Text Markings**

Passage 13: Clock Watching

1 B; *Sample answer:* I picked B because in the sentence where it appears, there are pairs of opposites. That helped me know that 'harried' is the opposite of calm, and 'frazzled' has the closest meaning.

2 D; *Sample answer:* I picked D because the other choices describe an event coming to an end.

3 *Sample answer:* I think it is quirky not just because a clock is narrating, but also because the clock has opinions, makes inferences and draws conclusions, like people do. It even claims to have a heart.

4 *Sample answer:* I think it takes place in a big city, perhaps London/New York because of the large crowds of people coming and going, and the entertainers pretending to be famous London/New York City landmarks.

Bienvenue, Mr Lindbergh!

Read the historical fiction story.
Then follow the instructions in the Text-Marking box.

It was a good thing Marcelle's family had left early for the airfield, since the traffic jam was the worst Paris had ever seen. Thousands were gathering on that summer night in 1927, eager to witness history being made. Many car headlights remained on, ringing the grassy field with light, illuminating it for the brave pilot and his small, unstable plane. All eyes were on the night sky, and the buzz of excitement was palpable.

Charles Lindbergh circled the Eiffel Tower before making for the lit-up target north-east of the city. When, after more than 33 non-stop hours in the air, the bold aviator safely touched down at 10:22, he encountered a scene of instant pandemonium. Exultant people toppled a chain-link fence and raced across the field for a closer look at him and his *Spirit of St Louis*. Marcelle was among them.

"Wow," she exclaimed as she approached the monoplane. "Not only is it so tiny, all it's got is a cramped, one-seat cockpit and a single engine. Plus, it's covered only in fabric!"

"And look," her dad added, "there's no window in the front – he must've had to look out the side to see where he was going!"

While the family investigated the plane and others swarmed over it, grabbing what they could as souvenirs, hundreds of others thronged around the startled Lindbergh. The exhausted hero seemed overwhelmed as they carried him off the field, tugging at his coat and yanking at his leather helmet. Marcelle swore she spotted the famous dancer Isadora Duncan among them, caught her eye and earned a smile.

When Marcelle finally got back home, she couldn't sleep, for witnessing the conclusion of the first transatlantic flight was the experience of a lifetime. But she didn't mind; Lindbergh hadn't slept either.

Text Marking

Use context clues to unlock meaning.

○ Circle the words:
illuminating, palpable, pandemonium, exultant and **thronged.**

▭ Box the expression:
caught her eye.

___ Underline context clues for each.

◀ **Sample Text Markings**

Passage 14: *Bienvenue,* Mr Lindbergh!

1 A; *Sample answer:* I picked A because the context clues helped me know that exultant means really excited.

2 D; *Sample answer:* I picked D because earlier in that sentence, the clue 'buzz of excitement' gave the idea that you could notice, even feel, how excited everyone was.

3 *Sample answer:* I think pandemonium involves lots of very excited, noisy, maybe frantic people at a momentous or unusual event or, perhaps, a frightening catastrophe where everyone is shocked, confused and scared.

4 *Sample answer:* According to the story, Lindbergh flew alone for 33 hours without sleep and was the first solo pilot to make a transatlantic flight. Furthermore, the plane was tiny, cramped, very flimsy and lacked a window in the front.

SCHOLASTIC

15 Compare & Contrast Name _____ Date _____

Under Review

Read the food story.
Then follow the instructions in the Text-Marking box.

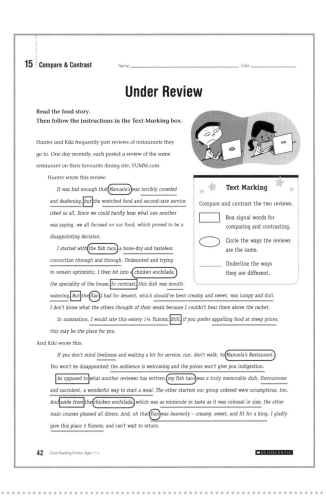

Hunter and Kiki frequently post reviews of restaurants they
go to. One day recently, each posted a review of the same
restaurant on their favourite dining site, YUMM.com.

Hunter wrote this review:

*It was bad enough that Manuela's was terribly crowded
and deafening, but the wretched food and second-rate service
irked us all. Since we could hardly hear what one another
was saying, we all focused on our food, which proved to be a
disappointing decision.*

*I started with the fish taco, a bone-dry and tasteless
concoction through and through. Undaunted and trying
to remain optimistic, I then bit into a chicken enchilada,
the speciality of the house. In contrast, this dish was mouth-
watering. But the flan I had for dessert, which should've been creamy and sweet, was lumpy and dull.
I don't know what the others thought of their meals because I couldn't hear them above the racket.*

*In summation, I would rate this eatery 1½ Yumms. Still, if you prefer appalling food at steep prices,
this may be the place for you.*

And Kiki wrote this:

*If you don't mind liveliness and waiting a bit for service, run, don't walk, to Manuela's Restaurant.
You won't be disappointed; the ambience is welcoming and the prices won't give you indigestion.*

*As opposed to what another reviewer has written, my fish taco was a truly memorable dish, flavoursome
and succulent, a wonderful way to start a meal. The other starters our group ordered were scrumptious, too.
And aside from the chicken enchilada, which was as miniscule in taste as it was colossal in size, the other
main courses pleased all diners. And, oh that flan was heavenly – creamy, sweet, and fit for a king. I gladly
give this place 3 Yumms, and can't wait to return.*

> **Text Marking**
>
> Compare and contrast the two reviews.
>
> ▢ Box signal words for comparing and contrasting.
>
> ◯ Circle the ways the reviews are the same.
>
> ___ Underline the ways they are different.

◄ Sample Text Markings

Passage 15: Under Review

1 C; *Sample answer:* I picked C because even though Hunter hated his first course, he summoned the courage to try the next dishes.

2 A; *Sample answer:* I picked A because each review mentioned slow or poor service.

3 *Sample answer:* Both reviewers went to the same restaurant on the same day and even ordered the same dishes.

4 *Sample answer:* People have different opinions. Many things are liked by some and disliked by others.

---

16 Compare & Contrast Name _____ Date _____

Theatres New and Old

Read the theatre story.
Then follow the instructions in the Text-Marking box.

Like his classmates, Zack was eager for the show to begin. They sat in
the Milton Keynes Theatre there to see *The Frogs*, a play by the Greek
playwright Aristophanes. Inside the theatre, most of the comfortable
seats were filled; the room was abuzz. The large, modern theatre,
which opened in 1999, was colourful and welcoming. Compared to
the storm raging outside, it was cosy.

On the same April day, Zack's aunt Viola was 3400 kilometres
away exploring the ancient outdoor theatre at Epidaurus, Greece.
That symmetrical stone venue, built nearly 2400 years ago,
was carved into a natural hillside, where warm spring breezes
rustled the leaves of trees that formed a living backdrop. This
amphitheatre, which can accommodate over 12,000 visitors on its
hard stone benches, is still used for plays and events. However, no
play was being performed that day.

Back in Milton Keynes, an announcer asked everyone to
turn off all electronic devices as the house lights dimmed. Actors
quietly entered to take their places. Zack took a last glance at his
programme and focused on the stage.

> **Text Marking**
>
> Compare and contrast the two theatre venues.
>
> ▢ Box signal words for comparing and contrasting.
>
> ◯ Circle ways the venues are alike.
>
> ___ Underline ways they are different.

The simple theatre at Epidaurus had no programmes, no speaker system and no house lights – just
daylight. Its most remarkable feature was its near-perfect natural acoustics. Viola's tour guide stood on
stage and spoke to visitors 30 rows away. Everyone could make out every word. By contrast, actors in Milton
Keynes wore body microphones to amplify their voices.

Zack enjoyed the centuries-old play performed in the Buckinghamshire venue. Meanwhile, his aunt
appreciated a centuries-old Greek venue with her tour guide as the sole performer, with perhaps a chorus of
ghosts for atmosphere.

◄ Sample Text Markings

Passage 16: Theatres New and Old

1 C; *Sample answer:* I picked C because the piece gives this information in paragraph 1. Also, I recognised what the other names referred to.

2 A; *Sample answer:* I picked A because I think the expression is more about excitement than about noise, so it seems the best answer.

3 *Sample answer:* Amphitheatres are open-air outdoor theatres, usually made of natural materials, while theatres like the one in Milton Keynes, are indoor theatres made of modern construction materials. An amphitheatre is a simpler, more natural setting, while an indoor theatre is likely to have modern conveniences.

4 *Sample answer:* No, Aunt Viola does not see a real play, but her tour guide does give a performance by standing on the stage and speaking to the visitors. The 'chorus of ghosts' refers to the actors who performed on the stage hundreds of years ago.

Answers

---

17 : Make Inferences   Name _____   Date _____

What, No TV?

Read the family story.
Then follow the instructions in the Text-Marking box.

When Enid and Gary got the news, they bubbled with excitement. Not everyone, they understood, gets to live in a real medieval castle. But they were about to. That's because their parents, both historians, volunteered to be the castle's caretakers for a year. The only bad part was really bad. They'd be so far from their friends.

As Maid Enid and Squire Gary began reading about castles, their eagerness to begin their stay grew. And when they stood for the first time before the towering, 800-year-old stone castle, replete with impenetrable walls, slits for windows and crenelated towers, their anticipation rose to new heights. They exuberantly crossed the drawbridge into their new home.

The first few days brought glorious hours of exploring its great rooms and halls, its dark dungeons and imposing towers. But after a week, the fun began to dissipate in the face of the realities of castle life. The massive stone walls and remote location severely limited the reception for their electronic devices: no texting for a year. Plus, there was no TV. And despite fireplaces large enough to stand in, the rooms were dimly lit, damp and often cold. Besides being so 'middle-aged' and uncomfortable, the castle was enormous. When Benny the beagle scampered off, it took hours of searching every nook, stairway and secret passage to find him.

But the family survived their unusual year, keeping busy with the many tasks of daily living without electricity and running water. They also learned to gather firewood and build fires, pump water and prepare and preserve food. They found entertainment in playing games, telling stories and making music. Still, when their parents next considered a year on an icebreaker in the Arctic, first mates Enid and Gary got cold feet.

Text Marking

Make an inference: What can you say about this family?

____ Underline text clues.

Think about what you already know.

46 Close Reading Fiction Ages 11+

■SCHOLASTIC

◄ **Sample Text Markings**

Passage 17: What, No TV?

1 A; *Sample answer:* I picked A because their parents appear to enjoy having adventurous experiences.

2 B; *Sample answer:* I picked B using my knowledge of words. I thought about the root penetrate, the suffix 'able' and prefix 'im' to work out it literally means 'not able to penetrate'.

3 *Sample answer:* I think they were willing to try one year living in a very unusual, isolated place. But the thought of a second year so far from friends and familiar things was too much for them.

4 *Sample answer:* I think sometimes an exciting adventure can sound better in theory than it turns out to be in fact. Be careful what you wish for!

---

18 : Make Inferences   Name _____   Date _____

Bad Break

Read the realistic fiction story.
Then follow the instructions in the Text-Marking box.

Ursula, a good student and talented artist, planned to attend art school to improve her skills. But her summer plans were in jeopardy when, walking her dog in May, she tripped over the lead, landed badly and broke her right leg. The moulded plaster cast Ursula wore home from the hospital immobilised her leg from knee to ankle. She'd wear it for eight weeks while finishing the school year.

Ursula returned to school a few days later using crutches. She was strong, but found that navigating busy corridors and the canteen proved more awkward than she'd expected. Like any child would be, Ursula was uncomfortable with this new reality. Although classmates freely offered to carry her books, bring things for her and help her get in and out of chairs, she always resisted, insisting, "No thanks, I'm fine." Embarrassed to feel weak and needy, she rejected help whenever it was offered.

Things changed one day in art class, where students were collaborating to paint a mural. The project demanded sharing equipment and lots of bending and reaching. Fretting that she'd feel useless, maybe even mess up the mural, Ursula asked Mr Wells to excuse her to sketch by herself at her desk. "You have lessons to learn right here, Ursula," the teacher gently suggested.

"What can I learn from messing everything up?" she asked sharply.

"You could learn to let others help you," replied Mr Wells. "There's no shame in needing help. We all want to support you, and you should learn to accept kindness." With the sweep of his arm, Mr Wells accidentally knocked a clipboard off his desk. Ursula reached out with her crutch and gently nudged it towards him. Mr Wells smiled. Ursula, experiencing an *Aha!* moment, smiled back.

Text Marking

Make an inference: How does the story reveal Ursula's personality?

____ Underline text clues.

Think about what you already know.

48 Close Reading Fiction Ages 11+

■SCHOLASTIC

◄ **Sample Text Markings**

Passage 18: Bad Break

1 C; *Sample answer:* I picked C because I think the 'new reality' is Ursula being temporarily disabled and embarrassed to need or accept help.

2 D; *Sample answer:* I picked D because I think the story is about the change in Ursula's abilities as a result of her accident and her reluctance to accept help.

3 *Sample answer:* I think her frustration and sense of helplessness boiled over when Mr Wells wouldn't let her sketch alone at her desk. She was hoping to escape the embarrassment she'd feel in the group project.

4 *Sample answer:* I think she automatically helped Mr Wells when his clipboard fell and appreciated his gratitude. That may have signalled to her that helping works two ways: it benefits the person who needs help, and it allows the helper to feel useful and appreciated, too. This experience may help Ursula become more accepting of her 'new reality'.

■SCHOLASTIC

Worksheet 19

Name _____ Date _____

Musical Finale

Read the music story.
Then follow the instructions in the Text-Marking box.

Alyssa Linton had always been a musical child. Her mother bragged that her daughter sang before she spoke, that she picked out melodies on the family piano before she ever took lessons. So it made sense that Alyssa cultivated that early fascination for anything she could use to make music. Her voice was her first instrument. Then came piano, recorder and accordion. She hoped to begin guitar lessons to expand her musical capabilities.

One June, the Linton family organised a reunion for relatives from around the country. Nearly seventy people came, representing five generations! On the reunion's last evening, everyone gathered in the party room of a local restaurant for a festive farewell dinner. People wearing name tags were seated at round tables, where laughter and conversation flowed easily. Alyssa sat at a table with children mostly her age. Though the talk was lively and friendly, Alyssa got distracted by the many water glasses near her.

On a whim, she tapped hers with a spoon and noticed that it rang out with a clear, pleasing tone. She began asking people to lend her their water glasses so she could entertain the whole table. Puzzled, relatives sipped some water and passed their glasses to Alyssa.

One by one, Alyssa adjusted the amount of water in each glass to create a musical scale of twelve distinct notes. Once she'd tuned and arranged the glasses, Alyssa began playing melodies by tapping them. The others at the table stopped talking to listen with delight, soon requesting tunes for Alyssa to try. In no time, she was tapping with two spoons to play melody and harmony!

Before long, relatives at other tables started making their own water-glass instruments. Within moments, the room sounded like a carnival with people of all ages singing, playing, clapping and dancing!

Text Marking

Summarise the story.

⬭ Circle the main idea.

___ Underline important details.

◀ **Sample Text Markings**

Passage 19: Musical Finale

1 B; *Sample answer:* I picked B because the theme of music runs through the whole story and Alyssa's music-making at the reunion party gets everyone involved and happy.

2 D; *Sample answer:* I picked D because I think that Alyssa's set of tuned water glasses is most like a xylophone because players tap on tuned wooden bars to play melodies.

3 *Sample answer:* According to the story, she was always interested in making music and imagined a way to use those glasses to create an instrument.

4 *Sample answer:* At the big party, Alyssa used her musical abilities and creativity to bring everyone together to sing, clap, play and dance.

Worksheet 20

Name _____ Date _____

Caving

Read the adventure story.
Then follow the instructions in the Text-Marking box.

Have you ever had an experience that was unnerving while it was happening, but when speaking of it later on, you retell it as a wonderful adventure? My friends and I did when we took a guided tour of a lava tube at the base of an extinct volcano.

"Listen carefully!" said Dan, our guide. "A lava tube is a cave formed by flowing lava that has hardened and cooled. Some of these natural underground conduits are long and large enough for caving. But others can be cramped and difficult to enter and explore, like parts of this one. But I see that you've got good hiking shoes and bright torches, so let's go!"

We giggled, gulped and followed Dan down into the darkness. After clambering down between sharp stalagmites and ducking under the perilous, icicle-like stalactites, we reached a room-sized chamber. It was smooth underfoot and walking was easier. Side tubes beckoned, so Dan led us into one, cautioning, "Slow and steady, cavers."

This tunnel quickly narrowed until we found ourselves crawling and squirming, getting scratched in the process. Despite Dan's confident assertion that all was well, we felt scared. So, we were relieved when he recognised that wriggling wasn't our thing, and led us back to the main chamber. It was slow-going, and what was creepy about it got even creepier when we heard a rustling sound behind us. "Just a bat," Dan advised. Nonetheless, that sound got us and our scraped knees scrambling out as fast as we could.

When I tell this caving story today, I speak of it as a thrilling escapade, fun from beginning to end. In fact, despite the presence of a qualified guide, we were all nervous, and never happier to be safely above ground.

Text Marking

Summarise the story.
Think about its theme.

⬭ Circle the main idea of the story.

___ Underline important details.

◀ **Sample Text Markings**

Passage 20: Caving

1 B; *Sample answer:* I picked B because Dan has just explained that they are going through a lava tube made by flowing lava, and he uses the word conduit to describe the same thing.

2 D; *Sample answer:* I picked D because in the story stalactites are described as things the spelunkers had to duck under.

3 *Sample answer:* I think that although the caving experience the author describes was actually frightening, the author prefers to remember it fondly as a great adventure.

4 *Sample answer:* I think the author wants to get across the idea that the group was covering up how nervous they felt about climbing down into darkness, even with an experienced guide.